Your Freelance Retirement

Practical Steps to Financial Security in the Gig Economy

Matilda Graham

Independently Published

First edition

Disclaimer: Please note that financial regulations, tax laws, and contribution limits are subject to change. While every effort has been made to ensure the accuracy of the information presented, the examples and figures used in this book reflect data available at the time of writing (referencing tax years 2024–2026). The IRS adjusts contribution limits and tax brackets annually for inflation, and legislation such as the SECURE 2.0 Act may alter rules in future years. Readers are responsible for verifying current financial figures, contribution limits, and tax regulations with the IRS or a qualified financial advisor before making financial decisions. If legal advice or other expert assistance is required, the services of a competent professional should be sought.

About the Author

Matilda Graham

Matilda Graham is a financial educator for the self-employed who believes you shouldn't need a calculus degree to manage your money. After spending over fifteen years navigating the unpredictable world of freelance work—from lean startup years to building sustainable income streams—Matilda knows firsthand that traditional employment guides simply don't work for the gig economy.Throu gh her personal experience managing irregular income and funding health insurance independently, she developed practical strategies that rely on basic, back-of-the-napkin math rather than complex formulas. She specializes in helping gig workers, freelancers, and solopreneurs simplify their retirement planning and taxes, proving that you don't need a boss to build wealth, you just need a better system.

Contents

Introduction

I'll never forget the moment I realized traditional retirement advice was completely useless for people like me. I was sitting across from a financial advisor who kept asking about my "employer match" and my "annual salary" concepts that meant nothing to someone cobbling together income from three different freelance clients, two contract gigs, and the occasional side project. When I tried to explain that my income last month was $6,200, but this month might be $3,800 or $9,500, depending on when clients paid their invoices, she looked at me like I was speaking a foreign language.

That's when I understood: the entire retirement planning system was built for a world that no longer exists for millions of us. A world of steady paychecks, employer-sponsored 401(k)s, automatic contributions, and someone else handling the complicated stuff. But if you're driving for Uber, freelancing as a designer, consulting independently, or running any kind of gig-based business, you're navigating retirement planning in a completely different landscape—one where the old maps don't work.

This book exists because I spent over fifteen years figuring out what does work. I've lived through the feast-or-famine income cycles, the quarterly estimated tax payments that always seemed to come at the worst possible time, and the anxiety of funding my own health insurance while trying to save for a retirement that felt impossibly far away. I've made mistakes—plenty of them—and I've also discovered strategies that work for people whose income arrives irregularly and who don't have an HR department to hold their hand.

Here's what I learned: you don't need a finance degree or complex formulas to build retirement security as a self-employed worker. You need practical systems that work with irregular income rather than against it. You need to understand the specific retirement account options designed for people like us—Solo 401(k)s, SEP-IRAs, and Roth accounts that offer more flexibility than traditional employer plans. You need realistic numbers for healthcare costs before Medicare kicks in at sixty-five, because that gap can destroy even the best-laid retirement plans. And you need to know when to claim Social Security, how to sequence your withdrawals to minimize taxes, and how to create a plan that survives market downturns and life's inevitable surprises.

This book breaks down every piece of the retirement puzzle into manageable steps you can implement immediately, whether you're twenty-five and just starting out or fifty-five and playing catch-up. We'll calculate your actual retirement number based on your real expenses, not generic formulas that assume everyone needs the same amount. We'll build savings systems that work with variable cash flow instead of requiring perfect consistency. We'll tackle the healthcare bridge that terrifies most early retirees. And we'll create withdrawal strategies that preserve your wealth throughout a retirement that could last thirty or forty years.

You'll notice this book uses real numbers, specific examples, and practical worksheets rather than vague encouragement. That's intentional. You deserve concrete guidance, not motivational platitudes.

You'll also notice we address different income levels and life situations throughout—because someone earning thirty-five thousand dollars faces different challenges than someone earning ninety thousand, and someone starting at forty-seven needs different strategies than someone starting at twenty-eight.

The truth is you can build a secure retirement without an employer-sponsored plan. You can retire comfortably—maybe even early—as a freelancer, gig worker, or self-employed professional. You just need a roadmap designed specifically for your reality, not someone else's. Let's build that roadmap together.

Let's start by assessing where you are in knowledge.

Quiz: The Freelancer's Retirement Reality Check

Instructions: Choose the answer that best describes your current relationship with money and retirement planning. Be honest, there is no HR department watching!

1. You find an online retirement calculator, and it asks for your "Employer Match %." What is your reaction?

- **A.** I type in "0" and feel a pang of jealousy for my corporate friends.

- **B.** I close the tab immediately. This tool clearly wasn't built for me.

- **C.** I laugh. My "employer match" is me buying myself a nicer coffee on Fridays.

- **D.** I try to calculate what my freelance rate "match" would be, get confused, and give up. (Context: Traditional calculators ask for fields like "employer match" and "annual salary" that make no sense to freelancers.)

2. A client pays you a lump sum of $6,000. What is your first thought?

- **A.** "I'm rich! Time to book that weekend getaway."
- **B.** "I should save some of this... but I have so many bills to catch up on from last month's dry spell."
- **C.** "Okay, that's really $3,500 after taxes, $500 for health insurance, and $2,000 for rent. I'm actually broke."
- **D.** "I'll put $1,000 in savings, but I'll probably have to transfer it back to checking next week." (Context: The "Triple Burden" means a $6,000 check isn't actually $6,000; it must cover taxes, healthcare, and retirement before living expenses.)

3. When someone asks, "When do you plan to retire?", you say:

- **A.** "Never. Writers/Designers/Consultants don't retire; we just fade away."
- **B.** "65? Isn't that the rule?"
- **C.** "Ideally 55, but I have no idea how I'll pay for health insurance before Medicare kicks in."
- **D.** "Whenever my bank account matches the scary number in my head." (Context: Freelancers often expect to retire later due to income volatility and the terrifying "healthcare gap" before Medicare at age 65.)

4. How do you currently save for retirement?

- **A.** I have a savings account that I raid whenever a client pays late.

- **B.** I try to save a fixed amount (like $500) every month, but I usually skip it during slow months.

- **C.** I wait until tax season to see if I have anything left over to dump into an IRA.

- **D.** I don't. I'm focusing on building my business revenue first. (Context: Traditional advice to "save a fixed amount" fails when income swings from $2,800 to $9,200 month-to-month.)

5. Which of these keeps you up at night the most?

- **A.** The tax bill I know is coming but haven't saved for.

- **B.** The fear that I'll have to go back to a "real job" just for the benefits.

- **C.** Paying $1,400+ a month for health insurance when I'm 60.

- **D.** All of the above. (Context: The "Triple Burden" of taxes, healthcare, and retirement funding is the primary source of anxiety for self-employed workers.)

Scoring Your Reality Check:

- **Mostly A's or D's:** You are in the **"Feast or Famine" Trap**. You are treating your freelance income like a salary, which creates anxiety when the numbers fluctuate. You need the **Percentage Method** (Chapter 4) to stop fighting your income swings.

- **Mostly B's:** You are stuck in the **"Employee Mindset."** You are trying to apply traditional rules (fixed savings, age 65 retirement) to a non-traditional career. You need to switch to **Variable Withdrawal Strategies** and the **Solo 401(k)** (Chapter 3).
- **Mostly C's:** You are a **"Freelance Realist."** You understand the math (and the pain) of self-employment tax and healthcare costs, but you lack a system to manage them efficiently. You are ready for the **Healthcare Bridge Fund** (Chapter 5) and **Tax Coordination Strategies** (Chapter 6).

The Good News: If you felt seen by these questions, this book was written specifically for you. We aren't going to use generic calculators or vague advice. We are going to build a system that works with your reality, not against it.

Chapter One

The Freelancer's Retirement Reality: Why Traditional Advice Doesn't Work for Gig Workers

Blake stared at the retirement calculator on his laptop screen, watching the numbers turn an alarming shade of red as he entered his income from freelance graphic design. The tool kept asking for his "employer match percentage" and "annual salary," fields that made absolutely no sense for someone who'd been cobbling together client projects for the past seven years.

This moment of frustration is where thousands of freelancers, gig workers, and self-employed professionals find themselves every single day. You've built a business, created income streams, and achieved the freedom that comes with being your own boss. But when it comes to retirement planning, every resource seems designed for someone else, with a steady paycheck, an HR department, and an employer who automatically deducts retirement contributions from every paycheck.

Traditional retirement advice doesn't just fail to help self-employed workers; it actively excludes us. The entire system was built around the assumption of lifetime employment with a single company, predictable income, and employer-sponsored benefits. When financial experts cheerfully advise you to "max out your employer match" or "take advantage of your company's pension," they're speaking a language that doesn't apply to your reality.

But here's what they don't tell you: being self-employed doesn't mean you're locked out of retirement security. In fact, you have access to retirement account options that many traditional employees can only dream about. You can contribute more to retirement accounts than most W-2 workers. You have greater control over your tax strategy. And you can design a retirement timeline that fits your actual life rather than conforming to corporate retirement ages.

The challenge isn't that retirement planning is impossible for freelancers; it's that you need a completely different approach. You can't simply work harder at following advice designed for traditional employees. You need strategies specifically built for irregular income, self-funded healthcare, and the unique tax situation of 1099 workers.

This chapter will show you why the traditional retirement system leaves self-employed workers behind and what that means for your planning approach. We'll explore the three fundamental ways that freelance retirement planning differs from traditional employment:

the income rollercoaster that changes how you save, the triple burden of funding your own retirement, healthcare, and taxes simultaneously, and the absence of employer safety nets that requires you to build your own security systems.

You'll discover that the obstacles you face aren't personal failures or signs that you've chosen the wrong career path. There are structural challenges built into a retirement system designed for a world that no longer exists for millions of Americans. More importantly, you'll learn that these challenges come with hidden advantages, flexibility, control, and opportunities that traditional employees don't have access to.

Whether you're 25 and just starting your freelance journey, 45 and realizing you need to get serious about retirement, or 55 and worried you've started too late, this chapter will help you understand why conventional retirement wisdom doesn't work for you, and what will work instead. You don't need to fit yourself into a system designed for someone else. You need to understand your unique situation and build a retirement plan that reflects the reality of self-employment.

Let's start by examining exactly why the employer-centric retirement system fails gig workers, and what you can do about it.

The Employer-Centric Retirement System: Why It Leaves Freelancers Behind

The retirement system in America was built on a simple premise: you work for a company, that company takes care of your retirement, and when you reach 65, you collect your pension and Social Security. This model worked beautifully for the post-World War II generation, when the average worker spent decades with the same employer and could count on a defined benefit pension that paid a fixed monthly amount for life.

But that world has vanished for most workers, and it never existed at all for freelancers and gig economy professionals.

The modern retirement infrastructure still operates as if stable, long-term employment is the norm.[6] Employer-sponsored 401(k) plans remain the primary vehicle through which Americans save for retirement, with the system designed around automatic payroll deductions, employer matching contributions, and HR departments that handle all the administrative complexity. According to the Congressional Research Service, workplace retirement plans are still "the primary way workers accumulate retirement savings," and access to these plans is almost entirely controlled by employers.[6]

When you're self-employed, you're locked out of this entire system by default.

You don't have an employer to sponsor a 401(k). You don't have automatic payroll deductions that make saving effortless. You don't have an HR department to explain your options, help you enroll, or remind you to increase your contributions. Most critically, you don't have an employer match, that "free money" that traditional employees receive when they contribute to their retirement accounts.

Instead, you must play three roles simultaneously: employee, employer, and plan administrator. You must research and choose your own retirement account type from a confusing array of options. A traditional IRA, Roth IRA, SEP-IRA, SIMPLE IRA, solo 401(k), or defined benefit plan. You must set up the account yourself, navigate the paperwork, and ensure you're complying with contribution limits and tax rules.[1 2 4] And you must fund both the "employee" and "employer" portions of your retirement savings from the same pool of income that also needs to cover your rent, health insurance, and quarterly tax payments.

The data shows exactly how this structural exclusion plays out in real life. Research from Pew Charitable Trusts on nontraditional workers, including freelancers, independent contractors, and gig workers, found that these workers are far less likely than traditional employees to participate in any retirement plan and often have little or no retirement savings beyond what they might eventually receive from Social Security.[5 6] Many nontraditional workers aren't saving anything for retirement at all, not because they don't understand its importance, but because the system makes it extraordinarily difficult to do so without employer infrastructure.[3 5]

This isn't a personal failing. It's a design flaw.

The employer-centric model assumes you have steady paychecks that arrive like clockwork, making it easy to commit to regular contribution amounts. But your income as a freelancer swings wildly from month to month. In March, you might earn $3,200. In April, $8,500. In May, $4,100. How do you set up automatic contributions when you don't know what next month's income will be?[1 3] The system offers no good answer because it wasn't designed with this question in mind.

The model also assumes someone else, your employer, will handle the cognitive load of retirement planning. They'll choose the plan provider, negotiate the fees, provide investment options, and send you educational materials. As a freelancer, all of that falls on you, on top of running your actual business, finding clients, sending invoices, and managing your taxes.[6]

This is why traditional retirement advice fails gig workers so completely. When financial experts tell you to "maximize your employer match" or "make sure you're enrolled in your company's 401(k)," they're speaking a language that doesn't apply to your reality. You need an entirely different playbook, one designed specifically for workers who must build their retirement security without any employer infrastructure to support them.

The Income Rollercoaster: How Irregular Earnings Change Everything About Saving

I learned this lesson the hard way during my third year of freelancing. In March, I earned $2,800, barely enough to cover rent and groceries. Then, in April, $9,200 came from three projects that all wrapped up simultaneously. I felt rich for exactly one week before realizing I had no system for turning that windfall into consistent retirement savings. By the time May arrived with another lean $3,400, the April money had evaporated into catch-up bills, a new laptop I'd been putting off, and meals out because I was too exhausted to cook.

This is the income rollercoaster that defines self-employment, and it changes absolutely everything about how you save for retirement.

Traditional retirement advice assumes you earn roughly the same amount every month. "Save 15% of every paycheck," the experts say, as if you receive paychecks. "Set up automatic transfers on payday," they suggest, as if you have a consistent payday. But when your income swings from $2,800 one month to $9,200 the next, then back down to $3,400, those tidy formulas collapse completely.

The psychological impact of this volatility is just as damaging as the mathematical challenge. Research on financial decision-making shows that income uncertainty triggers a scarcity mindset, in which you focus on immediate survival rather than distant goals like retirement.[8] When you don't know if next month will bring $3,000 or $8,000, your brain prioritizes keeping cash available for emergencies over locking it away in retirement accounts you can't easily access.

This explains why so many freelancers with decent annual incomes have almost nothing saved for retirement. It's not that you're irresponsible or don't understand compound interest. It's that the system for building retirement wealth was designed for people with predictable paychecks, and you're trying to force your irregular income into a framework that doesn't fit.

The data confirms this reality. According to research from the American Academy of Actuaries, gig workers and independent contractors often struggle with "day-to-day financial needs, emergencies, and lack of access to information on retirement savings strategies."[8] The MacroMonitor survey found that gig workers expect to retire three years later than traditional employees at age 67 versus 64, largely because income volatility makes consistent saving nearly impossible without specialized strategies.[7]

The problem compounds when you consider that freelancers must also manually set aside money for quarterly taxes.[7 8] Unlike employees, who have taxes automatically withheld from every paycheck, you receive your full payment and must exercise willpower to not spend the portion that belongs to the IRS. When a $5,000 client payment hits your account, it doesn't feel like you have $3,500 available after taxes; it feels like you have $5,000, and the temptation to spend it all is enormous.

Add in the irregular business expenses that come with self-employment, a new computer, software subscriptions, marketing costs, professional development, and retirement contributions, become the thing you'll "get to next month" when income is better.[8] Except next month brings its own challenges, and the pattern repeats.

This isn't a personal failing. It's a structural mismatch between how you earn money and how the retirement system expects you to save it.[7 8] The good news is that once you understand this fundamental difference, you can build saving strategies specifically designed for the income rollercoaster rather than fighting against it. The key is abandoning the fixed-dollar approach that works for salaried employees and embracing percentage-based systems that automatically scale with your variable income, saving more in abundant months and less in lean ones, but never stopping completely.

The Triple Burden: Funding Your Own Retirement, Healthcare, and Taxes Simultaneously

When I received my first $6,000 client payment after going freelance, I felt like I'd finally made it. Then reality hit: I owed $918 in self-employment tax, $450 for that month's health insurance premium, and I hadn't contributed anything to retirement in three months because I'd been "waiting for a good month." That single payment needed to cover all three obligations plus my actual living expenses. I sat at my kitchen table doing the math and realized I had about $3,200 left for rent, groceries, and everything else. The "big payment" suddenly felt very small.

This is the triple burden that defines self-employment, and it's the single biggest reason why traditional retirement advice fails freelancers so completely.[9 10 11]

When you work a traditional job, your employer handles much of this complexity invisibly. They automatically withhold your portion of payroll taxes; you never see that money, so you never miss it. They typically pay half of your health insurance premium, making coverage affordable. And many offer retirement plan matches, effectively giving you free money for saving. The cognitive load is minimal because the systems run automatically in the background.[9 10 11]

As a self-employed worker, you must manually juggle all three burdens from the same pool of income, with no employer subsidies and no automatic systems to help you.[9 11]

The Self-Employment Tax Reality

Let's start with the tax burden, because it's often the most shocking for new freelancers. Traditional employees pay 7.65% of their wages in

Social Security and Medicare taxes, while their employer pays the other 7.65%. You see only your half deducted from your paycheck.

When you're self-employed, you pay both halves, the full 15.3 % self-employment tax on your net earnings.[9 10] This is before you even calculate your regular income tax. If you earned $60,000 in net self-employment income last year, you owe approximately $9,180 in self-employment tax alone, plus whatever income tax applies to your bracket.

Unlike employees who have taxes automatically withheld, you must set this money aside yourself and pay it quarterly.[9 10] There's no system forcing you to do it, which means that a $6,000 client payment feels like $6,000 available to spend, until the tax bill arrives and you realize $918 of it was never really yours.

The Healthcare Premium Shock

The second burden is healthcare, and it hits harder than most freelancers expect.[10 11] According to 2024 data, the average individual marketplace premium for a 40-year-old is approximately $450 to $650 per month, depending on your state and the plan you choose. That's $5,400 to $7,800 annually that comes directly out of your pocket, with no employer contribution.

For a freelancer earning $50,000 annually, healthcare premiums alone consume 11% to 16% of gross income before you've saved a single dollar for retirement. If you're in a high-cost state or you're older, premiums increase significantly, and the percentage climbs even higher.

This creates an impossible trade-off: pay for comprehensive health coverage and have less available for retirement savings or choose a high-deductible plan to free up cash but risk financial catastrophe if you get sick.

The Retirement Funding Gap

The third burden is retirement itself. Without an employer match, every dollar in your retirement account must come from your own income, income that's already been reduced by self-employment taxes and health insurance premiums.[9 11]

If you're trying to save the commonly recommended 15% of your income for retirement, you're setting aside 15% of what's left after taxes and healthcare. On $60,000 in gross self-employment income, after $9,180 in self-employment tax and $6,000 in health premiums, you have roughly $44,820 remaining. Saving 15% of your original $60,000 means contributing $9,000 annually, but that's actually 20% of your after-tax, after-healthcare income.

This is why the triple burden is so devastating. You're not just saving for retirement, you're funding retirement, healthcare, and taxes simultaneously from the same limited pool of irregular income, with no employer subsidies to ease the pressure.[9 10 11] Traditional retirement advice that assumes employer benefits and steady paychecks simply doesn't account for this reality.[9 10 11]

Moving Forward: Building Your Own System

Blake's frustration with that retirement calculator wasn't a sign that he was failing at retirement planning; it was a sign that the retirement planning system was failing him. And if you've felt that same frustration, you're not alone. Millions of freelancers, gig workers, and self-employed professionals face the exact same disconnect between traditional retirement advice and the reality of their working lives.

The employer-centric retirement system wasn't designed with you in mind. It was built for a world of lifetime employment, steady paychecks, and employer-sponsored benefits, a world that's rapidly disappearing for traditional workers and never existed at all for the self-employed. When every calculator asks for your "employer match" and every article assumes you have automatic payroll deductions, it's easy to feel like retirement security is simply out of reach for people like us.

But here's the truth that changes everything: being self-employed doesn't lock you out of retirement security. It just means you need different strategies tailored to irregular income, self-funded healthcare, and the unique tax situation of independent workers.

The three fundamental challenges we've explored in this chapter, the employer-centric system that excludes you, the income roller-coaster that makes consistent saving difficult, and the triple burden of funding retirement, healthcare, and taxes simultaneously, aren't personal failures. They're structural obstacles built into a system designed for a different era. Understanding these obstacles is the first step toward overcoming them.

Throughout the rest of this book, you'll discover specific strategies that work for self-employed workers. You'll learn how to calculate your personal retirement number based on your real expenses and income level, not generic formulas. You'll discover retirement account options designed specifically for freelancers that offer higher contribution limits than traditional 401(k)s. You'll develop systems to consistently save that work with your irregular income, rather than fighting against it. And you'll create a comprehensive plan that coordinates retirement savings, tax strategy, healthcare coverage, and Social Security timing into one cohesive roadmap.

The advantages of self-employment, flexibility, control, and higher earning potential extend to retirement planning once you understand how to leverage them. You can contribute more to retirement accounts than most traditional employees. You have greater control over your tax strategy. You can design a retirement timeline that fits your actual life rather than conforming to corporate retirement ages. These advantages are real, but they only become accessible when you stop trying to force your freelance reality into a system designed for traditional employment.

Whether you're 25 and just starting your freelance journey with nothing saved, 45 and realizing you need to get serious about retirement planning, or 55 and worried you've started too late, the strategies in this book will show you how to build meaningful retirement security on your own terms. You don't need an employer to retire comfortably. You don't need a pension or automatic payroll deductions. You just need the right strategies, implemented consistently, with systems designed specifically for the reality of self-employment.

The retirement calculator that frustrated Blake wasn't asking the wrong questions, it was asking questions designed for someone else. In the chapters ahead, you'll learn to ask the right questions for your situation and build answers that actually work for the life you've chosen as a self-employed professional. Your retirement security isn't someone else's responsibility. It's yours, and that's your greatest advantage.

Chapter Two

Calculating Your Number: How Much Self-Employed Workers Actually Need to Retire

Hannah had been freelancing as a content writer for eight years when her father asked her a simple question over Sunday dinner: "So, what's your retirement number?" She froze mid-bite, realizing she had absolutely no idea whether it was a million dollars, two million, or if she could retire on less.

If you've ever felt that same stomach-dropping sensation when someone asks about your retirement plans, you're not alone. For self-employed workers, calculating how much they need to retire feels like trying to solve a puzzle with half the pieces missing. Traditional retirement calculators assume you have an employer match, a steady salary, and predictable expenses. They ask questions that don't apply to your life and give you answers that don't reflect your reality.

This chapter cuts through the confusion and gives you a practical, back-of-the-napkin method to calculate your personal retirement number, the actual dollar amount you need saved to retire comfortably on your terms. We're not talking about generic rules like "save ten times your salary" or "you need $2 million to retire." Those one-size-fits-all formulas ignore the messy reality of freelance life: the irregular income, the self-funded healthcare costs, and the fact that your "salary" changes every single year.

Instead, you'll learn how to work backward from your real expenses to find your target number. We'll start with what you actually spend today, adjust for the costs that will disappear in retirement and the ones that will increase, and then factor in the healthcare premium that most retirement guides conveniently ignore, the cost of individual market insurance during those critical years between when you want to retire and when Medicare kicks in at 65.

The beauty of this approach is that it's personalized to your life, not some theoretical average American. If you're comfortable living on $40,000 a year, your number will be dramatically different from someone who needs $80,000 annually. If you plan to retire at 60 instead of 67, that changes everything about how much you need to save. And if you're willing to work part-time in early retirement or adjust your lifestyle during market downturns, you can retire on significantly less than someone who needs absolute certainty and zero flexibility.

Throughout this chapter, we'll walk through real examples at different income levels and life stages. You'll see how a 28-year-old freelance designer earning $52,000 calculates their number differently from a 51-year-old consultant earning $95,000. You'll learn why your retirement number isn't a single fixed target but rather a range based on the lifestyle choices you're willing to make. And you'll discover that the healthcare gap between early retirement and Medicare eligibility can add $90,000 to $150,000 to your retirement number, a reality that most retirement advice glosses over but that self-employed workers must plan for explicitly.

By the end of this chapter, you won't just have a vague sense that you should "save more." You'll have your number—or more accurately, your range of numbers based on different retirement scenarios. You'll understand exactly what assumptions that number is based on and how to adjust it as your income, expenses, and goals change over time. Most importantly, you'll have transformed retirement from an overwhelming abstraction into a concrete, calculable target that you can work toward.

Your retirement number isn't a mystery that only financial advisors with complex software can solve. It's a straightforward calculation based on your real life, your actual expenses, and your specific goals. Let's figure out yours.

The Freelancer's Retirement Formula: Moving Beyond the 4% Rule

You've probably heard of the 4% rule—the idea that you can safely withdraw 4% of your retirement savings in your first year of retirement, adjust that amount for inflation each year after, and your money should last about 30 years.[14] [15] [16] It's simple, it's memorable, and for freelancers, it's dangerously incomplete.

The 4% rule came from research analyzing traditional retirements: people who worked steady jobs until 65, had pensions and employer benefits, and needed their savings to last until around 95.[14 15 16] That's not your situation. As a self-employed worker, you're facing a longer potential retirement if you want to stop working before 65. You have no pension to fall back on, and your Social Security benefits might be lower or more irregular due to your variable income history.[12 14 16]

Here's what the 4% rule doesn't account for in your freelance reality: You might retire at 58, not 65, meaning your money needs to last 40 years instead of 30. You'll likely continue earning some income in "retirement" because freelance skills don't just evaporate; you can take on projects when you want or need to.[13] Your expenses won't stay fixed; you'll cut back in lean years and spend more when markets are strong, because you've already lived that way throughout your career.[14 16]

Let me share what happened during my own planning. I calculated my retirement number using the standard 4% rule and felt confident I had enough saved. Then I realized I was planning to retire at 60, not 65. That extra five years before Medicare meant not only a longer retirement horizon but also significantly higher healthcare costs during the gap years. Suddenly, my "enough" wasn't enough anymore.

The freelancer's retirement formula starts with the 4% rule, but adapts it to your specific circumstances. If you're retiring before 65, consider using a 3% to 3.5% withdrawal rate as your baseline instead of 4%.[12] That lower percentage accounts for the longer time horizon and gives your portfolio more room to weather market downturns in those critical early years.

But here's where it gets interesting for freelancers: you can use a higher withdrawal rate if you build in flexibility.[12 13] Let's say you need $45,000 annually to cover your core expenses—housing, food, healthcare, utilities. Using a 3.5% withdrawal rate, you'd need about $1.29 million saved. But if you're willing to earn $10,000 to $15,000 annually from occasional freelance projects during your first decade of retirement, you only need your portfolio to provide $30,000 to $35,000. That drops your target to roughly $860,000 to $1 million, a difference of $290,000 to $430,000.

This is the power of the freelancer's formula: it acknowledges that your retirement won't be a hard stop. You'll likely downshift rather than quit entirely, taking on projects you enjoy without the pressure of needing a full-time income. This flexibility means you can retire earlier with less money or retire more comfortably with the same amount.

The formula also accounts for spending flexibility.[13 14 16] Separate your expenses into three buckets: essential (can't cut), adjustable (can reduce by 10-20% if needed), and discretionary (can eliminate entirely in bad years). If 60% of your spending is truly essential, you only need your portfolio to guarantee that amount using the conservative 3% to 3.5% rate. The remaining 40% can use a higher withdrawal rate because you can adjust it based on market performance.

Your freelancer's retirement formula isn't a single percentage. It's a range based on how much flexibility you're willing to accept and how much you'll realistically earn after "retiring." That range gives you options, and options give you security in a way that rigid rules never can.

The Healthcare Premium: Adding Pre-Medicare Insurance Costs to Your Number

When I first calculated my retirement number at age 44, I made the same mistake most freelancers make: I forgot about healthcare. I'd carefully tallied my living expenses, factored in inflation, and felt confident about my target. Then a friend who'd retired early at 58 casually mentioned she was paying $1,400 per month for health insurance, just for herself. That single conversation added $84,000 to my retirement number.

Here's the reality: if you plan to retire before age 65, when Medicare kicks in, you need to add a separate line item to your retirement calculation specifically for health insurance.[17 18] This isn't part of your regular living expenses; it's a distinct, substantial cost that can make or break your early retirement plans.[17 18 1]

Let's work through the math with real numbers. Say you're 60 and want to retire, but Medicare doesn't start until 65. That's five years of coverage you need to fund entirely on your own. Individual market health insurance for someone in their early sixties typically runs $800 to $1,500 per month, depending on your state, the plan type, and whether you qualify for subsidies through the Affordable Care Act marketplace.[17 18]

Using a middle estimate of $1,200 per month, that's $14,400 in premiums alone per year. Multiply that by five years, and you're looking at $72,000. But premiums are only part of the story.[17 18] You also need to budget for deductibles, copays, and out-of-pocket costs.[18] A bronze-level ACA plan might have a $7,000 deductible, while a silver plan might run $1,400 monthly but include a $3,000 deductible.[18] If you actually use healthcare, and most people in their sixties do, you could easily spend $18,000 to $22,000 annually when you combine premiums with expected medical costs.

Over that five-year gap, you're looking at $90,000 to $110,000 in total healthcare expenses before Medicare. That's a significant chunk of your retirement savings that needs to be earmarked specifically for staying insured and healthy.

Now here's where it gets interesting for self-employed workers: you have more control over this number than you might think. The ACA marketplace offers premium tax credits based on your income, not your assets.[18] If you structure your retirement income strategically, living primarily off Roth IRA withdrawals or taxable accounts with low capital gains, you can keep your Modified Adjusted Gross Income low enough to qualify for substantial subsidies.[18 1]

I've seen freelancers with $600,000 in retirement savings qualify for premium credits that reduced their monthly insurance costs from $1,300 to $400 by carefully managing their taxable income to stay within subsidy ranges.[18] That difference—$900 per month or $10,800 annually—can reduce your five-year healthcare gap cost from $110,000 to perhaps $40,000.

The key is to model this explicitly when calculating your number. Don't just add healthcare to a generic "living expenses" category.[17 18 1] Create a separate calculation:

Healthcare Gap Years = (Years until Medicare) × (Annual premium + Expected out-of-pocket costs - Estimated ACA subsidies)

For someone retiring at 58, that's seven years of coverage. At 60, it's five years. At 62, it's three years. Each scenario requires a different amount set aside specifically for healthcare.

When you add this healthcare premium to your retirement number, you're not being pessimistic; you're being realistic. The freelancers who successfully retire early are the ones who plan for this gap explicitly, get actual insurance quotes for their age and location, and build that cost into their target from day one.[1] The ones who struggle are those who assume healthcare will somehow "work itself out" or who drastically underestimate what individual market coverage actually costs.

Your retirement number isn't complete until you've added the healthcare premium. It might be the difference between thinking you need $800,000 and realizing you really need $950,000. But knowing that number now means you won't be blindsided later.

Your Personal Calculation: Working Backward from Real Expenses to Find Your Target

The most powerful retirement calculation you can do doesn't start with investment returns or savings rates. It starts with your grocery bill, your rent payment, and your actual life. This backward approach cuts through the noise and gives you a number based on reality, not theory.[20]

Here's how it works: grab your bank statements from the last three months and a notebook. You're going to track every dollar you spent, but with a critical distinction that most retirement calculators miss. Separate your expenses into three categories: costs that will disappear in retirement, costs that will stay the same, and costs that will increase.

In the "disappear" column, list everything tied to working. For me, that was my coworking space membership at $220 monthly, professional liability insurance at $95 monthly, and the roughly $180 I spent each month on client lunches and coffee meetings. When you stop working full-time, these vanish. Add them up, that's money you won't need your retirement savings to cover.

The "stay the same" category includes your core living expenses: housing, utilities, groceries, car insurance, phone bill, and basic entertainment. This is your baseline. For most freelancers I've worked with, this number falls between $2,800 and $5,500 per month, depending on location and lifestyle. Don't judge your number against anyone else's; a freelancer in rural Ohio has different costs than one in Seattle.

Now the hard part: the "increase" column. This is where healthcare lives, and it's the line item that derails more early retirement plans than any other.[19] If you're currently paying $450 monthly for marketplace insurance, understand that premiums typically increase with age. A 45-year-old might pay $550 monthly for the same coverage that costs a 60-year-old $1,200 monthly. You need to research actual quotes for your age at retirement, not assume your current rate will hold.

Let's work through a real example. Say you're 42 years old, planning to retire at 60, and your current annual expenses break down like this:

- Work-related costs that disappear: $6,000
- Core living expenses that continue: $48,000
- Current healthcare: $5,400
- Estimated healthcare at age 60-65: $14,400 annually

Your retirement spending need is $48,000 plus $14,400 in healthcare, totaling $62,400 annually. But here's where it gets interesting, you don't need to fund all of that from savings if you're willing to earn some income.[19 20]

If you take on occasional freelance projects earning $15,000 annually during your early retirement years, you only need your portfolio to provide $47,400. Using a conservative 3.5% withdrawal rate, that means you need approximately $1.35 million saved. But if you want to stop working entirely, you'd need about $1.78 million to safely withdraw that full $62,400.

This is your range, not a single fixed number. The beauty of working backward from expenses is that you can immediately see how different choices affect your target.[19] Willing to relocate somewhere with lower housing costs and save $800 monthly? Your retirement number drops by roughly $274,000. Planning to delay retirement until 65 and eliminate that expensive pre-Medicare healthcare gap? You might need $300,000 less.

Your personal calculation isn't about hitting some guru's recommended number. It's about understanding exactly what your life costs, what it will cost in retirement, and how much capital you need to generate that income sustainably.[20] Once you have that number, everything else in your retirement plan falls into place. Conclusion: your number is a starting point, not a finish line

Hannah eventually found her retirement number; in reality, she found three of them. She had her lean number ($950,000 for a minimal lifestyle), her comfortable number ($1.4 million for her current spending), and her abundant number ($1.8 million for travel and splurges). Having that range transformed her anxiety into action because she finally understood what she was working toward.

Your retirement number isn't a single, fixed destination that you either hit or miss. It's a range based on the choices you're willing to make about when you retire, how much you'll spend, whether you'll earn any income after "retiring," and how much flexibility you can tolerate. The freelancer who needs absolute certainty and zero lifestyle adjustments requires a much larger number than someone comfortable adapting their spending to market conditions or taking on occasional projects.

The calculations we've covered in this chapter, the modified withdrawal rates, the healthcare premium additions, and the backward-from-expenses approach, give you a personalized target based on your actual life, not some theoretical average American. If your number feels impossibly large right now, remember that you have decades to build toward it, and every dollar you save today compounds into significantly more by retirement. If your number feels surprisingly achievable, that's the power of understanding your real expenses rather than assuming you need some arbitrary million-dollar milestone.

What matters most isn't whether your number is $800,000 or $1.5 million; it's that you know your number and understand what assumptions it's based on. You know how much of your spending is truly essential versus adjustable. You've factored in the healthcare gap that derails so many early retirement plans. You've considered whether you'll earn any income in retirement, which can dramatically reduce how much you need to save. And you've built in the flexibility that makes retirement sustainable for self-employed workers who've spent their careers adapting to irregular income.

Your number will change as your life changes. As your income grows, you might raise your target to maintain a higher standard of living in retirement. If you decide to relocate to a lower-cost area, your number might drop by $200,000 or more. As you get closer to retirement and have better data about your actual spending patterns and healthcare costs, you'll refine your calculations. That's not a flaw in the system; that's exactly how retirement planning should work for freelancers whose income and circumstances evolve constantly.

The most important step you can take right now is to calculate your baseline number using the methods in this chapter. Pull out your bank statements, separate your expenses into categories, research healthcare costs for your target retirement age, and work backward to find your target. It might take an hour or two, but that investment of time will give you clarity that transforms retirement from an overwhelming abstraction into a concrete, achievable goal.

Once you have your number, the next question becomes: how do you build wealth toward that target when you're self-employed? That's where retirement accounts designed specifically for freelancers and gig workers become your most powerful tools, accounts that offer higher contribution limits and better tax advantages than anything available to traditional employees. Let's explore those options next and figure out which ones make the most sense for your specific situation and income level.

Chapter Three

DIY Retirement Savings: Choosing Between Solo 401(k)s, SEP-IRAs, and Roth Accounts

Savannah had been driving for a rideshare company for three years, supplementing that income with weekend food-delivery gigs, when her tax preparer asked whether she'd opened a retirement account yet. She laughed and said, "I thought those were only for people with real jobs," not realizing she had access to retirement savings options that many corporate employees could only dream of.

This misconception, that retirement accounts are exclusively for traditional employees with steady paychecks, keeps countless gig workers, freelancers, and independent contractors from building the wealth they deserve. The truth is exactly the opposite: as a self-employed worker, you have access to more powerful retirement savings tools than most W-2 employees will ever see. You can contribute more money, enjoy greater tax benefits, and maintain complete control over your retirement strategy. The catch? You have to set it up yourself, and you need to understand which account type makes sense for your specific situation.

This chapter cuts through the alphabet soup of retirement accounts—Solo 401(k)s, SEP-IRAs, and Roth accounts—and shows you exactly how to choose the right option based on your income level, how much you can realistically save, and how much administrative complexity you're willing to handle. We're not going to drown you in tax code or make you feel like you need an accounting degree to make a decision. Instead, you'll learn the practical differences between these accounts in plain language, with real numbers that show what each option means for someone earning $35,000 versus someone earning $85,000.

The Solo 401(k) offers the highest contribution limits, potentially allowing you to save over $60,000 annually if your income supports it, by letting you contribute both as the employee and the employer of your own business. It's the powerhouse option for serious savers who want to maximize their tax-deferred retirement savings and don't mind a bit of extra paperwork. The SEP-IRA offers simplicity and flexibility, making it ideal for freelancers with fluctuating income who want an easy setup without annual filing requirements, though its contribution limits are lower than those of a Solo 401(k) at the same income level. Roth accounts—whether a Roth IRA or Roth Solo 401(k)—offer tax-free growth in retirement, which can be incredibly valuable if you're younger, currently in a lower tax bracket, or expect your income to increase significantly over time.

Here's what most retirement planning guides won't tell you: you don't necessarily have to choose just one. Many self-employed workers strategically combine account types, contributing to a Roth IRA for tax-free growth while also funding a Solo 401(k) to reduce current taxes. The key is understanding how each account works, what the contribution limits mean in dollars you can save, and which combination makes sense for your current income and future goals.

Through Savannah's story, you'll see how a gig worker making $52,000 annually discovered she could save nearly $30,000 in tax-advantaged retirement accounts—far more than her corporate friends with their employer-sponsored plans. You'll learn the specific steps to open each type of account, understand the real-world trade-offs between simplicity and maximum contributions, and discover how to coordinate multiple account types if that strategy makes sense for you.

By the end of this chapter, you'll know exactly which retirement account to open, how much you can contribute based on your actual income, and how to set it up this week—not someday when you have it all figured out, but right now, with the income and circumstances you actually have. The biggest mistake isn't choosing the "wrong" account type; it's waiting another year to start saving while you try to make the perfect decision.

The Solo 401(k): Maximum Contributions for Serious Savers

When Savannah's tax preparer mentioned the Solo 401(k), she pulled out a simple chart showing contribution limits that made Savannah's eyes widen. "You could have put away nearly $30,000 last year," the preparer explained. "That's not a typo; it's how the Solo 401(k) works when you're both the employee and the employer."

The Solo 401(k) is the heavyweight champion of retirement accounts for self-employed workers who want to save aggressively. Unlike a SEP-IRA, which only allows employer contributions, a Solo 401(k) lets you contribute in two distinct ways: as the employee of your business and as the employer.[27] This dual contribution structure is what makes it possible to save far more than most corporate employees can put into their company 401(k)s.

Here's how the numbers work for 2025. As the employee, you can defer up to **$23,500** of your income into the Solo 401(k), the same limit that applies to any 401(k) plan.[24] This is money that comes directly from your business income before you pay income tax on it, reducing your current tax bill. Then, as the employer, you can contribute an additional amount based on your business structure: roughly **25% of your W-2 wages** if you operate as an S-corporation or C-corporation, or about **20% of your net self-employment income** if you're a sole proprietor or single-member LLC (after accounting for the self-employment tax deduction).[28 27]

The total combined limit for 2025 is **$70,000** if you're under 50, or **$77,500** if you're 50 or older and making catch-up contributions.[24 23 26] For 2026, these limits increase to **$72,000** and **$80,000** resp ectively.[26 21 24] These are the highest contribution limits available to self-employed workers, period.

Let's translate this into real scenarios. If you earned $60,000 in net self-employment income last year, you could contribute the full $23,500 as an employee deferral, plus roughly $11,000 as an employer contribution (about 20% of your net earnings after adjustments), for a total of approximately $34,500. That's 58% of your income going into tax-deferred retirement savings—far more than the typical corporate employee saving 10% or 15%.

If you earned $100,000, you could max out the employee deferral at $23,500 and add about $18,500 in employer contributions, reaching roughly $42,000 in total contributions. To hit the full $70,000 limit, you'd need net self-employment income of around $190,000 or higher, depending on your exact business structure and deductions.[23]

The catch-up contributions for those 50 and older add another **$7,500** in 2025 (increasing to **$8,000** in 2026).[24 25] Even better, if you're between ages 60 and 63, you qualify for a "super catch-up" of **$11,250** under the SECURE 2.0 Act—giving late-career freelancers an extra boost to accelerate their retirement savings.[24 21 22]

The trade-off for these massive contribution limits is slightly more complex than a SEP-IRA. You'll need to adopt a formal plan document (many providers offer free templates), and once your account balance exceeds $250,000, you'll need to file a simple annual form with the IRS. For serious savers, this modest administrative burden is a small price to pay for the ability to shelter tens of thousands of additional dollars from taxes each year.

The Solo 401(k) also offers flexibility that SEP-IRAs don't: you can choose to make your employee contributions as traditional pre-tax deferrals or as Roth contributions, giving you control over whether you want to reduce taxes now or enjoy tax-free withdrawals in retire ment.[24] You can even split your contributions between both types in the same year.

The SEP-IRA: Simple Setup for Fluctuating Income

If the Solo 401(k) is the heavyweight champion for maximum contributions, the SEP-IRA is the reliable workhorse. It's simple, flexible, and perfectly designed for freelancers whose income swings wildly from month to month. When I first started freelancing, I opened a SEP-IRA specifically because I had no idea what I'd earn in any given year. Some months brought in $8,000 in client payments; others,

$2,000. The SEP-IRA let me wait until tax time to decide how much I could afford to contribute[29 31 34], rather than committing to a fixed amount when my income was still a moving target.

The beauty of a SEP-IRA is its radical simplicity. You can set one up in about twenty minutes with most major brokerages, often using a single-page form.[29 32] There's no annual filing requirement with the IRS[31 35], no complex plan documents to maintain, and virtually no ongoing administrative burden.[35] For a freelancer juggling client deadlines and invoices, this minimal paperwork is a genuine advantage; you're not adding another complicated system to manage on top of running your business.

Here's how the contribution structure works: unlike the Solo 401(k), which allows both employee and employer contributions, a SEP-IRA allows only employer contributions.[30 33] As a self-employed person, you're the employer, so you can contribute up to **25% of your net self-employment income** (after accounting for the self-employment tax deduction), with a maximum of **$69,000 for 2024**.[30 32] In practice, the calculation works out to roughly **20% of your net earnings** for most sole proprietors.[36 32]

Let's translate that into real numbers. If you earned $50,000 in net self-employment income last year, you could contribute approximately $10,000 to your SEP-IRA. If you earned $80,000, you could put away about $16,000. If you had an exceptional year and earned $150,000, you could contribute around $30,000. The contribution scales automatically with your income—higher earnings mean higher potential contributions, but you're never locked into a specific amount.

The game-changing feature for freelancers with variable income is this: **you don't have to contribute every year**.[32] If you have a terrible year where you barely cover expenses, you can skip your

SEP-IRA contribution entirely without penalty or paperwork.[30 32] If the following year is fantastic, you can make a large contribution to catch up.[30] This flexibility is exactly what gig workers need—a retirement account that works with the feast-or-famine reality of self-employment rather than demanding consistent contributions you can't always afford.

Even better, you can open a SEP-IRA and make contributions **up until your tax filing deadline, including extensions**, potentially as late as October 15th for the previous tax year.[29 31 34] This means you can finish your year, calculate your actual income, prepare your taxes, and then decide exactly how much to contribute based on what you can afford and what will optimize your tax situation. Try doing that with a corporate 401(k).

The trade-off for this simplicity is lower contribution limits compared to a Solo 401(k) at the same income level. That $50,000 earner could only put away $10,000 in a SEP-IRA, versus potentially $23,500 in employee deferrals alone with a Solo 401(k). There are also no catch-up contributions for those over 50[30], and no Roth option—SEP-IRA contributions are always pre-tax[32], with taxes due when you withdraw in retirement.

For freelancers earning under $60,000 annually, or those who value simplicity over maximum contributions, or anyone whose income fluctuates so dramatically that committing to regular contributions feels impossible, the SEP-IRA is often the perfect fit. It's the account that says: contribute what you can, when you can, without the pressure of complex rules or rigid requirements.

Roth Accounts: Tax-Free Growth for Long-Term Thinkers

The third option in your retirement account toolkit is the Roth account, either a Roth IRA or the Roth option within a Solo 401(k), and it works fundamentally differently from everything we've discussed so far. With traditional retirement accounts and SEP-IRAs, you get a tax break today and pay taxes later when you withdraw in retirement.[38 41] With Roth accounts, you flip that equation: you pay taxes on your contributions now, but every dollar of growth and every withdrawal in retirement is completely tax-free.[38 39 41]

For a 32-year-old freelancer, this tax-free growth can be extraordinary. Contribute $6,000 to a Roth IRA today, and if it grows to $45,000 over thirty years, you can withdraw all $45,000 in retirement without paying a single dollar in federal income tax.[38 39 43] Compare that to a traditional IRA, where you'd owe taxes on the entire $45,000 at whatever your tax rate is in retirement, potentially $10,000 or mo re.[38 41]

The Roth IRA has a contribution limit of **$7,000 for 2024** (or $8,000 if you're 50 or older), which is significantly lower than what you can put into a Solo 401(k) or SEP-IRA.[42] But what it lacks in contribution limits, it makes up for in flexibility and long-term advantages. You can also choose a Roth option within your Solo 401(k) if your provider offers it, allowing you to make some or all your employee deferrals as Roth contributions while still benefiting from the higher 401(k) contribution limits.[41]

Here's the strategic question every freelancer needs to answer. Should you pay taxes now (Roth) or later (traditional)? The answer depends largely on your current tax bracket versus your expected retirement tax bracket.[39 40] If you're early in your freelance career, earning $35,000 to $50,000 annually and paying a relatively low tax rate, Roth contributions can be brilliant. You're locking in today's low tax rate and creating a pool of money that will never be taxed again, even if tax rates increase or your income grows substantially.[39 40]

I learned this lesson the hard way in my early years as a freelancer. I was so focused on reducing my current tax bill that I put everything into traditional retirement accounts. Years later, when my income had grown, and I understood tax planning better, I realized I'd missed a golden opportunity. Those early years when I was in the 12% or 22% tax bracket were the perfect time to pay taxes on contributions, because I'll almost certainly be in a higher bracket when I retire and start drawing Social Security on top of retirement account withdrawals.[39 40]

Roth accounts also offer a unique safety valve for freelancers: you can withdraw your contributions (not the earnings) at any time, for any reason, without taxes or penalties.[37 39 40] If you contribute $7,000 this year and face a genuine emergency next year, you can pull that $7,000 back out.[40] This isn't ideal—you're robbing your future self—but it's there if you need it.[37 40 44] The earnings stay locked until age 59½ and must meet the five-year rule to be withdrawn tax-free, but your original contributions remain accessible.[38 39 40]

The Roth strategy becomes even more powerful when you think about required minimum distributions. Traditional IRAs and 401(k)s force you to start taking taxable withdrawals in your seventies, whether you need the money or not.[40 42] Roth IRAs have no required minimum distributions during your lifetime, meaning you can let that money grow tax-free for as long as you live, or leave it to your heirs as a tax-free inheritance.[40 42]

For younger freelancers and those currently in lower tax brackets, Roth accounts aren't just an option; they're often the smartest choice for building long-term, tax-free wealth.[39 40]## Taking Control: Your Retirement Account Action Plan

Savannah's story reveals a truth that transforms how self-employed workers should think about retirement savings: you're not locked out of the system. You have more options and greater control than most traditional employees will ever experience. The alphabet soup of retirement accounts isn't designed to confuse you; it's a toolkit specifically built to give independent workers the flexibility to save aggressively when income is strong and adjust when it's not.

The decision between a Solo 401(k), a SEP-IRA, and a Roth account isn't about finding the one "perfect" option that works for everyone. It's about understanding the trade-offs and choosing the account—or combination of accounts—that aligns with your current income, savings capacity, and the administrative complexity you're willing to handle. A 28-year-old freelance designer earning $45,000 might thrive with a Roth IRA for tax-free growth and a SEP-IRA for simplicity. A 52-year-old consultant earning $95,000 who wants to maximize contributions and catch up on lost time might choose a Solo 401(k) to take full advantage of those higher limits and catch-up contributions.

What matters most isn't which account you choose, it's that you choose one and open it this month, not next year when you think you'll have everything figured out. Savannah spent three years believing retirement accounts weren't for people like her, costing her thousands in lost contributions and years of compound growth she can never recover. The biggest mistake isn't opening a SEP-IRA when a Solo 401(k) might have been slightly better; it's waiting another year to start while you agonize over the decision.

Here's what you need to do in the next two weeks. First, calculate your net self-employment income from last year and determine how much you could realistically contribute to retirement based on the limits we've discussed. Be honest about what you can realistically afford, not what you wish you could save. Second, choose your account type using this simple framework: if you value simplicity and have fluctuating income, start with a SEP-IRA. If you want maximum contributions and don't mind modest paperwork, open a Solo

401(k). If you're younger or in a lower tax bracket, add a Roth IRA to whichever option you choose. Third, go to a low-cost brokerage that specializes in accounts for self-employed workers and complete the application—it will take less than an hour.

The retirement account you open this week won't be perfect, and that's completely fine. You can always adjust your strategy later, open additional accounts as your income grows, or switch from a SEP-IRA to a Solo 401(k) when higher contribution limits become relevant. What you can't do is recover the years you spend paralyzed by indecision, watching your corporate friends accumulate retirement wealth while you wait for the perfect moment to start.

Your retirement security doesn't depend on having an employer to automatically enroll you or match your contributions. It depends on understanding that you have powerful tools available right now, choosing the one that fits your current situation, and making your first contribution before the month ends. The account you open today, even if it's not the theoretically optimal choice, will serve you infinitely better than the perfect account you never get around to opening. Stop waiting for permission or perfect conditions. You're self-employed, which means you're already running a business. Now it's time to run your retirement the same way: with decisive action, realistic planning, and the confidence that comes from taking control of your financial future.

Chapter Four

Building Wealth on Irregular Income: Consistent Retirement Strategies for Variable Cash Flow

Thomas earned $8,200 in March, barely scraping together enough for rent and groceries from his web development projects. Then April arrived with $14,500 in client payments, and suddenly he felt rich—until he realized he had no system for turning these unpredictable windfalls into consistent retirement savings.

If you've ever experienced the freelancer's financial rollercoaster—where one month you're wondering how you'll pay rent and the next you're debating whether to splurge on that new laptop—you already understand the core challenge this chapter addresses. Traditional retirement advice assumes you receive a steady paycheck every two weeks, making it easy to set up automatic contributions and forget about them. But when your income swings from $3,000 one month to $12,000 the next, that advice becomes useless. You can't automate what isn't predictable, and you can't commit to fixed monthly contributions when you don't know what next month will bring.

This chapter tackles the most frustrating obstacle facing gig workers who want to build retirement wealth: how do you save consistently when your income is anything but consistent? The answer isn't to earn more money or to somehow magically smooth out your cash flow—it's to build systems that work with your income variability rather than against it.

You'll discover three practical strategies designed specifically for the feast-or-famine reality of self-employment. The percentage method shows you how to save a fixed percentage of every payment you receive, regardless of size, so your retirement contributions automatically scale with your income. Instead of trying to save $1,000 every month (which might be impossible in lean months and insufficient in abundant ones), you'll save 15% or 20% of whatever comes in—$150 from a $1,000 payment, $2,000 from a $10,000 payment.

The income smoothing buffer strategy teaches you how to create your own version of a steady paycheck by building a cash reserve that evens out the peaks and valleys. This buffer isn't your emergency fund; it's a separate account that captures excess income during good months and supplements your income during slow months, allowing you to maintain consistent retirement contributions even when client payments are erratic.

The baseline-plus strategy provides a framework for adjusting your savings rate based on your income each month. You'll establish a minimum contribution amount that you commit to even in your leanest months, then accelerate your savings when income is strong. This approach ensures you're always making progress toward your retirement goals while acknowledging that, for some months, you'll sprint and others, you'll walk.

Throughout this chapter, you'll see real numbers from actual freelance scenarios, what these strategies look like when you're earning $40,000 versus $80,000 annually, how to implement them when you're just starting out versus when you're established, and how to adjust them when life throws you unexpected expenses or income disruptions.

The most important insight you'll gain is this: irregular income doesn't have to mean irregular savings. With the right systems in place, you can build retirement wealth just as effectively as someone with a traditional paycheck, maybe even more effectively, because you have more control over your income potential. The key is stopping the cycle of "I'll save whatever's left over" and replacing it with strategies that ensure you're consistently paying your future self, regardless of what any individual month brings.

Let's build a system that turns your unpredictable income into predictable retirement security.

The Percentage Method: Saving a Fixed Percentage Regardless of Income Swings

The simplest and most powerful strategy for building retirement wealth on irregular income is also the most counterintuitive: stop trying to save the same dollar amount every month. Instead, commit to saving the same percentage of every payment you receive, no matter how large or small.

When I first started freelancing, I tried to save $500 monthly for retirement. In good months when I earned $6,000, that felt easy, almost trivial. But in lean months when I scraped together $2,800, that $500 felt impossible, and I'd skip it entirely, telling myself I'd "make it up later." I never did. The percentage method changed everything by eliminating that monthly negotiation with myself.

Here's how it works in practice. You choose a percentage, let's say 15%, and apply it to every single payment that hits your account, before you do anything else with that money. A client pays you $3,000? You immediately transfer $450 to your retirement account. The next client pays $800? You transfer $120. A big project pays $7,500? You move $1,125 to retirement. The dollar amounts vary wildly, but the habit stays constant.

This approach mirrors your actual income reality.[45 46] In months when you earn more, you save more. In months when you earn less, you save less—but you still save something. Over time, your retirement contributions automatically reflect your true earning pattern rather than fighting against it.

The percentage you choose matters, and it should be based on both your income level and how much time you have until retirement. If you're in your thirties with decades ahead of you, starting at 10-12% gives you room to increase later as your income grows.[47] If you're in your forties playing catch-up, you'll likely need 20-25% or more.[47] Someone earning $40,000 annually might realistically commit to 10%, while someone earning $85,000 could push toward 18-20% without dramatically impacting their lifestyle.

The key is choosing a percentage you can sustain even in your lower-earning months. Look at your income over the past year and identify your three lowest-earning months. Could you have saved your target percentage in those months and still covered your essential expenses? If not, adjust downward until you find a percentage that's realistic for your actual income floor, not your aspirational average.

Many freelancers find it helpful to layer their percentage on top of their tax savings. When a payment arrives, immediately move 25-30% to your tax savings account, then apply your retirement percentage to what remains. This ensures you're calculating based on money that's truly available for personal use rather than gross revenue that includes tax obligations.

The percentage method also creates natural opportunities for catch-up. That $12,000 project you landed? Your 15% rule automatically captures $1,800 for retirement, far more than you'd save in a typical month. These windfalls become built-in accelerators for your retirement savings rather than disappearing into lifestyle inflation or forgotten spending.

Start by implementing this rule for just three months. Track every payment you receive and the corresponding retirement contribution. You'll likely discover two things: first, that your total savings over those three months exceeds what you would have saved with a fixed monthly target, and second, that the mental relief of having a simple, non-negotiable rule eliminates the exhausting monthly debate about whether you can "afford" to save.[46 48]

The percentage method isn't about perfection, it's about creating a system that works with your reality instead of against it. Your income will always fluctuate as a freelancer. Your savings habit doesn't have to.

Building Your Income Smoothing Buffer: Creating Consistent Cash Flow from Irregular Payments

The percentage method gets you saving consistently, but there's still a problem: your monthly expenses don't fluctuate with your income.

Rent is due on the first, whether you earned $3,000 or $9,000 last month. Your health insurance premium doesn't adjust based on how many clients pay. This mismatch between variable income and fixed expenses is what keeps many freelancers in a constant state of financial anxiety, and what often derails retirement contributions when cash gets tight.

An income-smoothing buffer solves this by creating your own version of a steady paycheck.[50] Think of it as a holding tank that captures excess income during abundant months and releases funds during lean ones, transforming your feast-or-famine cash flow into something that feels remarkably like regular employment—except you're the one creating that stability.[50]

Here's the basic structure. You need three separate accounts: your business checking account, where all client payments land; a high-yield savings account that serves as your buffer; and your personal checking account for household expenses.[50 51] Every dollar you earn flows through this system in a specific sequence.

When a client payment hits your business account, you immediately move your tax percentage (typically 25-30%) to a dedicated tax savings account and your retirement percentage (the 10-20% we discussed earlier) to your retirement account.[49 50] What remains goes into your buffer account. Then—and this is the key—you pay yourself a fixed amount from the buffer to your personal checking on a set schedule, just like an employer would.[50]

Let's make this concrete with real numbers. Say you've calculated that you need $4,200 monthly to cover all your personal expenses, rent, food, insurance, car payment, everything.[50 51] That becomes your target monthly "salary." You set up automatic transfers of $2,100 on the 1st and 15th of each month from your buffer to your personal checking.[50] In March, you only earn $5,800 after taxes and retirement contributions, but you still pay yourself the full $4,200, drawing down your buffer by $1,600. In April, you earn $11,200 after those deductions, pay yourself the same $4,200, and your buffer grows by $7,000.

The target size for your buffer depends on how variable your income is and how risk-averse you are. I recommend starting with a goal of three months of expenses, in our example, that's $12,600.[49 50 51 52] If your income is highly seasonal or you have few anchor clients, push toward six months ($25,200).[49 50 51 52] This might sound like a huge amount to accumulate, but remember: you're building it during your high-earning months, not trying to save it all at once.[49]

Building the buffer initially requires discipline. For the first few months, you might need to live more leanly than your income would suggest, funneling every dollar of surplus into the buffer until you hit your target. Once it's established, the buffer maintains itself, growing in good months, shrinking in lean ones, but keeping your personal cash flow steady throughout.[50]

The psychological shift this creates is profound.[50 51 52] Instead of checking your bank balance before every purchase and wondering if you can "afford" your retirement contribution this month, you know exactly what you have available because your personal account receives the same predictable deposits every two weeks. The anxiety of irregular income doesn't disappear entirely, but it shifts from your daily life to a monthly number you check—your buffer balance—which is far more manageable.[50 51]

This system also protects your retirement contributions.[49 50] When a slow month hits, you're not choosing between paying rent and funding your Solo 401(k). Your buffer covers both, because you've already planned for this exact scenario.[49 50] The retirement contribution happened automatically when the income arrived, and your personal expenses are covered by your fixed salary from the buffer.[50]

The Baseline-Plus Strategy: Minimum Contributions in Lean Months, Accelerated Savings in Abundant Ones

The percentage method and income smoothing buffer work beautifully when you're established and earning consistently—but what about when you're just starting out, or when you hit a genuinely lean period that drains your buffer? This is where the baseline-plus strategy becomes essential, giving you a framework that acknowledges reality: some months you can barely contribute anything, and other months you can save aggressively.[53 54 1 55]

The baseline is your non-negotiable minimum, the smallest retirement contribution you commit to making even in your worst mont hs.[54 1 55] This isn't aspirational. It's the amount you can sustain when a major client disappears, when projects dry up, or when you face an unexpected expense that depletes your buffer. For many freelancers, this might be $100 to $300 monthly, depending on their income floor and essential expenses.

To find your baseline, look at your three lowest-earning months from the past year.[54 55] After covering absolute essentials—rent, food, minimum debt payments, health insurance—what could you have contributed to retirement without creating genuine hardship? That's your baseline. It might feel uncomfortably small compared to what financial experts say you "should" save, but remember: the goal is consistency, not perfection.[53 1] A $150 monthly baseline maintained for thirty years builds approximately $170,000 at 7% returns. Zero dollars saved in lean months because you set an unrealistic target builds nothing.

The "plus" component is where you make up ground. In months when your income exceeds your baseline needs, you accelerate contributions dramatically.[53 54 1 55] The specific formula varies by situation, but a common approach is to save 40-60% of all income above your baseline budget. If your baseline budget (including that minimum retirement contribution) is $4,000 and you earn $7,500 after taxes, you'd save an additional $1,400 to $2,100 beyond your baseline retirement contribution.

I implemented this during my third year of freelancing when my income ranged from $3,200 in February to $11,800 in November. My baseline contribution was $200 monthly, painful to admit given all the advice about saving 15-20%, but realistic for my situation. In the months when I earned under $5,000, I contributed only $200. In months earning $7,000 or more, I added 50% of everything above $5,000. That November, I contributed $3,600—my $200 baseline plus $3,400 from my abundant-month formula.

Over that year, I contributed $14,800 to retirement despite six months of barely scraping by. Without the baseline-plus framework, I would have contributed nothing in those lean months and probably spent the abundant months' surplus on lifestyle inflation rather than strategic savings.

The psychological benefit of this approach is profound. In lean months, you're not failing; you're executing your plan by maintaining your baseline. In abundant months, you're not just "doing better", you're implementing a predetermined strategy that ensures those windfalls translate into retirement security rather than evaporating into forgotten purchases.[53 1]

Track your contributions monthly and calculate a running annual total.[54 1 56] This helps you see whether your baseline-plus strategy is keeping you on track toward your yearly target. If you're consistently falling short, you have two levers to adjust: raise your baseline slightly if your income floor has increased, or increase the percentage you save from abundant months.[1 55] If you're exceeding your target, you can either maintain the aggressive pace to retire earlier or redirect some surplus to other goals.

The baseline-plus strategy isn't about having perfect months or perfect years. It's about building a system that works with the reality of freelance income: acknowledging that some months are survival mode while others are opportunities to sprint ahead, and that both are normal parts of building wealth without an employer.[53 1 55]

Creating Your Wealth-Building System

The strategies in this chapter—the percentage method, income smoothing buffer, and baseline-plus approach—aren't about choosing one perfect system and rigidly following it forever. They're about understanding the fundamental principle that makes retirement savings possible for freelancers: you need systems that work with your income variability, not against it.

Thomas's story illustrates what happens when you stop fighting the feast-or-famine cycle and start building around it. His income swings didn't disappear; March was still lean at $8,200, and November was still abundant at $15,200. But by implementing the percentage method and building his buffer, he transformed those swings from a source of constant anxiety into a manageable reality that no longer derailed his retirement contributions. The variability became predictable, which made it far less threatening.

The most important decision you'll make after reading this chapter isn't which specific percentage to save or how large to build your buffer. It's the decision to stop waiting for your income to stabilize before you start saving consistently. Your income will never stabilize—that's the nature of self-employment. But your savings habit can be rock-solid if you build the right framework.

Start with the percentage method this week. Choose a realistic percentage based on your actual income floor, not your aspirational average. If you've been earning $40,000 to $70,000 annually with significant monthly variation, begin with 10% and prove to yourself that you can maintain it for three months. You can always increase later, but you need to establish the habit first. Calculate that percentage for every payment you receive and transfer it immediately, before the money gets absorbed into your general spending.

If you're further along in your freelance career and have some savings already, add the income smoothing buffer as your next priority. You don't need to build the full three to six months of expenses before you start—begin with a goal of one month, then two, then three. Every dollar you add to that buffer reduces the stress of irregular income and protects your retirement contributions from being sacrificed during inevitable lean periods.

The baseline-plus strategy becomes essential when you're starting out, recovering from a setback, or facing genuinely variable income that makes even the percentage method feel unstable. Knowing your absolute minimum contribution: that $150 or $200 or $300 that you'll save even in your worst months, creates a floor that prevents you from backsliding to zero. And knowing your abundant-month formula ensures that good months translate into accelerated progress rather than lifestyle inflation.

These three strategies can be layered together or used individually, depending on your situation. A freelancer earning $35,000 annually might start with just the baseline-plus approach, establishing that minimum contribution and building from there. Someone earning $75,000 with established clients might implement all three simultaneously: the percentage method for consistency, the buffer for stability, and the baseline-plus framework for the occasional exceptional month or unexpected setback.

The irregular income that once felt like an insurmountable obstacle to retirement savings is just a logistics problem with practical solutions. You've learned those solutions in this chapter. Now the only question is: which one will you implement first? Not someday when your income is more stable, not next year when you've landed that dream client, but this week, with your very next payment.

Your retirement security doesn't require perfect income; it requires a system that works with the income you have. You now have that system. Use it.

Chapter Five

Healthcare Before Medicare: Bridging the Gap from Early Retirement to Age 65

Tessa had meticulously calculated her retirement number, planned her investment withdrawals, and even mapped out her Social Security claiming strategy, but she'd made one devastating miscalculation. At 58, she'd assumed health insurance would cost maybe $800 per month until Medicare kicked in at 65, when the actual quotes she received ranged from $1,400 to $1,900 monthly for decent coverage. That single oversight—underestimating healthcare costs by nearly $100,000 over seven years—threatened to derail fifteen years of disciplined retirement savings.

For self-employed workers dreaming of early retirement, healthcare represents the single largest obstacle between age 55 and 65. Unlike corporate employees who might have access to retiree health benefits or generous COBRA coverage, freelancers and gig workers face the individual insurance market entirely on their own. The premiums can be staggering, often consuming 20% to 30% of your entire retirement budget during those critical gap years. Yet most retirement calculators and planning guides treat healthcare as an afterthought, offering vague suggestions to "budget for insurance" without providing the concrete numbers and strategies you need.

This chapter tackles the healthcare gap head-on, giving you the practical tools to bridge the years between early retirement and Medicare eligibility at 65. You'll learn what individual market insurance costs at different ages and in different regions, because a 58-year-old in Arizona faces dramatically different premiums than a 58-year-old in New York. We'll break down how the Affordable Care Act marketplace subsidies work for retirees, and more importantly, how your retirement account withdrawal strategy directly affects your eligibility for those subsidies. Understanding this connection could save you tens of thousands of dollars.

We'll also explore the often-overlooked strategy of managing your retirement income specifically to maximize healthcare subsidies. Because marketplace subsidies are based on your Modified Adjusted Gross Income rather than your assets, you can have $500,000 in retirement savings but still qualify for substantial premium assistance if you're strategic about which accounts you withdraw from and when. This is where your Roth conversions, withdrawal sequencing, and healthcare planning intersect, and getting this coordination right can mean the difference between paying $1,500 monthly for insurance versus $400.

Beyond the numbers, this chapter addresses the psychological challenge of healthcare planning for early retirement. Many self-employed workers delay retirement not because they lack sufficient savings, but because they're terrified of the healthcare gap. That fear is valid; medical emergencies can devastate even well-funded retirement plans. But fear without a concrete plan keeps you working longer than necessary. Our goal is to transform that vague anxiety into a specific, manageable strategy with clear costs and realistic solutions.

You'll learn how to calculate your personal healthcare bridge fund, the extra money you need to set aside specifically for medical costs during the gap years. We'll show you how to evaluate different insurance plan types, understand deductibles and out-of-pocket maximums, and make informed trade-offs between monthly premiums and potential medical expenses. And we'll explore alternative strategies, such as part-time work for benefits, health-sharing ministries, and geographic arbitrage, that might reduce your healthcare burden.

Whether you're planning to retire at 55, 60, or 62, the healthcare gap is solvable. It requires planning, realistic budgeting, and strategic coordination with your overall retirement plan, but it's absolutely manageable. By the end of this chapter, you'll have a clear framework for bridging those critical years before Medicare, transforming healthcare from a retirement-killing obstacle into just another line item in your comprehensive early retirement strategy.

The Real Cost of Pre-Medicare Healthcare: What Individual Market Insurance Actually Costs by Age and Region

When I first started researching health insurance costs for my own early retirement planning, I made the same mistake most freelancers make: I looked at what I was currently paying—about $420 per month for a decent Silver plan at age 38—and assumed it would stay roughly the same, maybe creeping up to $600 or $700 by my early sixties. That assumption was wildly, dangerously wrong.

The reality of individual marketplace insurance is that your age becomes the single biggest factor in what you'll pay, and the increases aren't gradual; they accelerate dramatically as you approach Medicare eligibility. Under the Affordable Care Act, insurers can charge a 64-year-old up to three times what they charge a 21-year-old for the exact same coverage.[60] That's not a typo. Three times.

Let's talk about actual numbers, because vague warnings don't help you plan. Based on 2026 marketplace data, the national average premium for an individual buying coverage is around $680-$690 per month before any subsidies.[57 58] That's the baseline for a typical adult. But here's where age changes everything: if you're in your early fifties, you're likely looking at $700 to $900 monthly for a mid-level Silver plan in most regions.[57 58 59 60] By age sixty, that same coverage jumps to roughly $1,200 to $1,500 per month.[58 59 60] And if you're 62 or 63—just two or three years from Medicare—you could easily face premiums of $1,400 to $1,900 monthly for decent coverage.[58]

These are unsubsidized prices, which we'll address in the next section, but you need to understand the sticker price first because it determines how much subsidy help you might receive.

Geography matters almost as much as age. Your ZIP code has become the dominant factor in what you'll pay, sometimes even more influential than your age bracket.[59] A 60-year-old freelancer in Pittsburgh might find Gold plans—the second-highest tier with low deductibles—for around $353 per month at the base rate.[59] That same person in Providence, Rhode Island, could pay $521 monthly for comparable Gold coverage.[59] In some Kansas markets, Gold premiums jumped 68% in a single year, from $451 to $759 monthly.[59]

The regional differences aren't random. They reflect local healthcare costs, hospital pricing, the number of insurers competing in your area, and state-specific regulations.[60] Two states—New York and Vermont—prohibit age-based pricing entirely, meaning a 30-year-old and a 62-year-old pay identical premiums for the same plan.[60] That sounds fair until you realize the premiums themselves are often higher because costs are averaged across all ages.[60]

For freelancers planning early retirement, these numbers create a sobering reality check. If you're 58 and want to retire before 65, you're looking at seven years of premiums that could total $100,000 to $130,000 before subsidies, and that's just the premiums, not deductibles, copays, or out-of-pocket costs when you use healthcare.

The plan type you choose also significantly affects costs. HMO plans average about $674 monthly, while PPO plans, which offer broader networks and more flexibility, run around $789 monthly, roughly $115 more.[58] For location-independent freelancers who travel frequently or split time between states, that PPO flexibility might be worth the premium, but it's a real cost difference that compounds over multiple years.

Understanding these baseline costs is essential before we discuss subsidies and income management strategies, because you can't plan around something if you don't know what it costs. The healthcare gap isn't insurmountable, but it requires honest numbers and realistic budgeting, not wishful thinking about what insurance "should" cost.

Marketplace Subsidies and the ACA: How Retirement Income Affects Your Premium Tax Credits

Understanding the baseline cost of individual market insurance is only half the equation. The other half—often the difference between affordable early retirement and working until 65—is the Premium Tax Credit, a federal subsidy that can reduce your monthly premiums by hundreds or even thousands of dollars.[64] But here's the catch that trips up most early retirees: your eligibility for these subsidies depends entirely on your retirement income, not your assets.[65]

This creates a fascinating paradox for self-employed retirees. You could have $800,000 in retirement savings and still qualify for substantial premium assistance if you're strategic about how much taxable income you generate each year.[65] The Affordable Care Act's Premium Tax Credit is based on your Modified Adjusted Gross Income (MAGI) as a percentage of the Federal Poverty Line[64]—currently about $15,060 for a single person or $20,440 for a couple in the contiguous United States.[63] If your MAGI falls between 100% and 400% of the poverty line (roughly $15,000 to $60,000 for an individual, or $20,000 to $82,000 for a couple), you may qualify for subsidies that dramatically reduce your premiums.[61,62]

Here's where retirement income planning becomes critical. Every dollar you withdraw from a traditional IRA or 401(k) counts as taxable income and increases your MAGI.[62,65] The same goes for pension income, capital gains from selling investments, interest, dividends, and any part-time work earnings. But—and this is crucial—qualified withdrawals from Roth IRAs don't count toward MAGI at all.[65] Neither do withdrawals of your original contributions from taxable investment accounts (though the gains do count).

Let me give you a concrete example. Tessa, from our opening story, had planned to withdraw $45,000 annually from her traditional Solo 401(k) to cover her expenses from age 58 to 65. At that income level, she'd be at roughly 300% of the poverty line and would qualify for premium tax credits that could reduce her $1,500 monthly premium to around $520; a savings of nearly $12,000 per year, or $84,000 over seven years.[62]

But if Tessa had instead withdrawn $65,000 in one year to buy a car and fund a major trip, pushing her income above 400% of the poverty line, she'd lose her subsidy eligibility entirely for that year.[61 62] Under current law (which is scheduled to revert to pre-2021 rules after 2025), crossing that 400% threshold means you receive zero subsidy, not a reduced subsidy, but nothing at all.[61 62] That single year of higher income could cost her the full $18,000 in unsubsidized premiums, plus she'd have to repay any advance credits she'd already received.[61 62]

This is why withdrawal sequencing matters so much for early retirees. The optimal strategy often involves drawing primarily from Roth accounts and cash savings during your ACA years to keep your taxable income low and maximize subsidies.[65] You can supplement with small traditional account withdrawals if needed, but you want to stay well below that 400% cliff—ideally targeting 200% to 300% of the poverty line, where subsidies are substantial but you're not at risk of accidentally crossing the threshold.[62]

For freelancers with variable income histories, this requires careful annual planning.[65] You'll need to project your income each year when you apply for coverage, then monitor it throughout the year. If your actual income ends up higher than projected, you'll reconcile the difference on your tax return using Form 8962, potentially repaying some or all of the advance credits you received.[61 64] The key is building enough flexibility into your withdrawal strategy that you can adjust mid-year if needed, drawing less from traditional accounts and more from Roth or cash if you've had unexpected income.

Building Your Healthcare Bridge Fund: Calculating the Extra Savings Needed for the Gap Years

Now that you understand what healthcare costs and how subsidies work, it's time to calculate the specific dollar amount you need to set aside, your healthcare bridge fund. This isn't money sitting in your general retirement account, hoping to cover whatever comes up. It's a dedicated reserve, separate from your main retirement portfolio, earmarked specifically for medical costs during those gap years.[66]

Think of your healthcare bridge fund as having three distinct components: premiums, predictable out-of-pocket costs, and a buffer for the unexpected. Let's break down each piece with actual numbers.

Start with premiums. If you're planning to retire at 60 and you've determined that marketplace insurance will cost you $1,200 monthly after subsidies, that's $14,400 per year. Multiply by five years until Medicare kicks in at 65, and you're looking at $72,000 just for premiums. But healthcare costs don't stay flat—they typically increase 4% to 6% annually. Using a conservative 5% inflation rate, your actual five-year premium cost would be closer to $79,500. This is your baseline number.

Next, add your predictable out-of-pocket costs. Even with insurance, you'll face deductibles, copays, and coinsurance. Let's say you choose a Silver plan with a $4,000 deductible and an $8,500 out-of-pocket maximum. In a typical year where you're reasonably healthy, you might spend $2,000 to $3,000 on routine care, prescriptions, and minor issues, essentially half your deductible. Over five years, budget roughly $12,000 to $15,000 for these predictable costs, adjusted upward for medical inflation.

Here's where most people stop calculating, and that's a mistake. You need a buffer for the bad years—the unexpected surgery, emergency room visit, the specialist treatments that push you toward your out-of-pocket maximum. I recommend setting aside an amount equal to at least one full out-of-pocket maximum for your gap period. If your plan caps annual costs at $8,500, add another $8,500 to your bridge fund as insurance against a serious health event.

Let's put this together for our 60-year-old retiree planning a five-year bridge:

- Premiums (inflation-adjusted): $79,500
- Predictable out-of-pocket costs: $13,500
- Emergency buffer: $8,500
- Total healthcare bridge fund: $101,500

That's a sobering number, but it's realistic. And here's the critical part: this money should be held separately from your main retirement portfolio, ideally in low-risk investments like short-term bonds, CDs, or a high-yield savings account.[67 68] You cannot afford to have this fund drop 20% in a market correction right when you need to pay your premiums.[68]

If you have a Health Savings Account from your working years, those dollars should be counted first. They're tax-free for medical expenses and effectively reduce your bridge fund requirement dollar-for-dollar. If you have $30,000 in your HSA, you only need to save an additional $71,500 in after-tax money for your healthcare bridge.

For couples, the calculation becomes more complex. If you're both retiring at 60, you're essentially doubling most of these costs. Two premiums, two sets of out-of-pocket expenses. However, family plans often cost less than two individual plans, so research your specific marketplace options carefully.

The healthcare bridge fund isn't optional or negotiable; it's the price of admission for early retirement as a self-employed worker. But once you've calculated the real number and started building this dedicated reserve, the healthcare gap transforms from a vague source of anxiety into a concrete, manageable line item in your retirement plan.

Turning Healthcare Anxiety into a Concrete Plan

The healthcare gap between early retirement and Medicare eligibility at 65 is real, expensive, and often underestimated—but it's also completely solvable with the right planning. What separates successful early retirees from those who remain trapped in full-time work isn't necessarily having more money. It's understanding the actual costs, knowing how the subsidy system works, and building those expenses into your retirement number from the beginning, rather than treating healthcare as an afterthought.

Let's be clear about what we've learned: individual marketplace insurance for someone in their late fifties or early sixties can easily cost $1,200 to $1,900 monthly before subsidies. Over a seven-year gap from 58 to 65, that's potentially $100,000 to $160,000 in premiums alone. Add deductibles, copays, and out-of-pocket expenses, and you're looking at a six-figure line item in your retirement budget. These aren't scare tactics; they're the real numbers you need to plan around.

But here's the opportunity that most early retirement guides miss: the Premium Tax Credit system is specifically designed to help people with assets but modest income, exactly the situation of a self-employed early retiree. By strategically managing which accounts you withdraw from and how much taxable income you generate, you can potentially reduce those $1,500 monthly premiums to $400 or $500. That's not gaming the system; it's understanding how the system works and making informed decisions about Roth conversions, withdrawal sequencing, and income timing.

Your healthcare bridge fund, that dedicated reserve of $80,000 to $120,000, depending on your gap years, needs to be carefully planned as carefully as your main retirement portfolio. This isn't money that should be invested aggressively in stocks, where a market downturn could devastate it right when you need to pay premiums. It should be in stable, accessible investments that preserve capital while earning modest returns. Think of it as insurance for your insurance, the price you pay for the freedom to retire before 65.

The strategies we've covered in this chapter aren't theoretical. They're the same approaches that thousands of self-employed workers have used to successfully bridge the healthcare gap. Some, like Tessa, adjusted their retirement timeline to reduce the gap years. Others managed their income carefully to maximize subsidies. Still others found part-time work that offered health benefits or relocated to states with lower premiums and better marketplace options. There's no single right answer; there's only the answer that works for your specific situation, income level, and retirement goals.

What matters most is that you've transformed healthcare from a vague source of anxiety into a concrete, calculable expense with specific strategies to manage it. You know what insurance costs at different ages. You understand how subsidies work and how your withdrawal strategy affects eligibility. You can calculate your personal healthcare bridge fund and know exactly how much extra you need to save beyond your basic retirement number.

The healthcare gap is no longer the invisible obstacle that keeps you working longer than necessary; it's just another component of your comprehensive early retirement plan. Challenging, yes, but manageable with the right information and strategic planning. And that knowledge gives you something invaluable: the confidence to retire on your own terms, not when an employer decides you can have health benefits, but when you've built the systems and savings to provide for yourself.

The bridge to Medicare is crossable. You just need to know how much lumber to buy and where to place the supports. Now you do.

Chapter Six

Independent Contractor Tax Planning: Keeping More Money for Your Retirement

Alana watched her tax preparer's fingers fly across the keyboard, entering her freelance consulting income for the year. When the final number appeared on the screen, $14,872 in taxes owed, she felt physically sick, realizing she'd paid more in taxes than she'd managed to save for retirement all year. The tax bill wasn't just painful; it was a wake-up call that she'd been hemorrhaging money that could have been building her retirement instead. Like many freelancers, Alana had been treating taxes as something that happened to her once a year, a mysterious calculation performed by someone else that always seemed to result in owing more than she'd expected. What she hadn't realized was that every dollar unnecessarily paid to the IRS was a dollar that couldn't compound and grow in her retirement accounts for the next twenty or thirty years.

For self-employed workers, tax planning and retirement planning aren't separate activities, they're two sides of the same coin. The tax code provides significant advantages to independent contractors, but only if you understand how to use them. Home office deductions, mileage tracking, business expense documentation, and strategic retirement contributions can save thousands of dollars annually. Yet most freelancers leave this money on the table simply because no one ever explained how the system works or showed them what they're entitled to claim.

The challenge is that traditional tax advice assumes you're an employee with a W-2, a steady paycheck, and an employer handling half your payroll taxes. But as a 1099 worker, you're paying both the employee and employer portions of Social Security and Medicare taxes; that's 15.3% right off the top before you even calculate your income tax. This self-employment tax burden is one of the biggest shocks for new freelancers and one of the most misunderstood aspects of independent work. Many gig workers don't realize they can deduct the employer portion of this tax, or that strategic retirement contributions can significantly reduce their overall tax burden.

This chapter will show you how to keep more of your hard-earned money by understanding the tax strategies specifically available to self-employed workers. You'll learn how to calculate your true tax burden, so you're never surprised by a five-figure bill at tax time. We'll break down the most valuable deductions for independent contractors. From the home office deduction that many freelancers wrongly fear will trigger an audit, to mileage tracking that can save thousands annually, to business expense documentation that reduces your taxable income while supporting your business growth.

Most importantly, you'll discover how retirement contributions and tax planning work together to maximize your wealth building. Every dollar you contribute to a Solo 401(k) or SEP-IRA doesn't just build your retirement savings; it also reduces your current tax bill, creating a powerful double benefit. We'll show you how to coordinate your retirement contributions with your tax planning throughout the year, rather than scrambling at tax time to figure out how much you owe.

Whether you're earning $40,000 or $120,000 as a freelancer, the strategies in this chapter will help you implement a system for managing taxes proactively instead of reactively. You'll learn to set aside the right percentage of each payment for taxes, track deductible expenses systematically, and make strategic decisions about retirement contributions that reduce your tax burden while building long-term wealth. By the end of this chapter, you'll understand that keeping more money for retirement isn't about aggressive tax avoidance, it's about understanding the legitimate strategies the tax code specifically provides for self-employed workers and implementing them consistently throughout the year.

The Self-Employment Tax Reality: Understanding Your True Tax Burden and the Employer-Employee Split

When I first went freelance after years of corporate work, I thought I understood taxes. I'd been paying them my whole working life, after all. But my first quarterly estimated tax payment hit me like a freight train, not because the amount was huge, but because I suddenly realized I was paying taxes I'd never even seen before. My former employer had been quietly covering half my Social Security and Medicare taxes, and now that invisible benefit had vanished. I was on the hook for the full 15.3% self-employment tax[72 70 73], plus my regular income tax. It felt like someone had changed the rules without telling me.

Here's what happens when you're self-employed: you pay both sides of the payroll tax equation. As a traditional employee, you pay 7.65% of your wages for Social Security and Medicare, 6.2% for Social Security, and 1.45% for Medicare.[70] Your employer matches that with another 7.65%, bringing the total to 15.3%.[70] You never see that employer contribution on your paycheck, but it's real money being paid on your behalf. When you become self-employed, you become both the employee and the employer[72], which means you're responsible for the entire 15.3%.[72 70]

This isn't a penalty or some unfair burden placed on freelancers; it's simply the same system applied differently. The Social Security and Medicare programs need to be funded regardless of how you earn your income. But understanding this split is crucial because it dramatically affects how much money you have available for retirement savings and living expenses.

Let's break down the math with a concrete example. Say you earned $80,000 in net profit from your freelance business last year. You don't pay self-employment tax on the full $80,000—the IRS applies it to 92.35% of your net earnings[70 72], which accounts for the fact that the employer half is technically a business expense. So, your self-employment tax base is $73,880. Multiply that by 15.3%, and you owe $11,304 in self-employment tax alone, before calculating your income tax.

Now here's the part that softens the blow slightly: you can deduct half of your self-employment tax—the employer-equivalent portion—when calculating your adjusted gross income.[72 70] In this example, that's roughly $5,652. This deduction doesn't reduce your self-employment tax itself, but it does reduce the income that's subject to federal income tax[72 70], which saves you money depending on your tax bracket. If you're in the 22% bracket, that deduction saves you about $1,243 in income tax.

The Social Security portion of the self-employment tax applies only up to a wage base that adjusts annually for inflation. For 2026, that cap is $184,500.[71] Once your net earnings exceed that threshold, you only pay the 2.9% Medicare portion on the excess.[69 71] High earners face an additional 0.9% Medicare tax on self-employment income above $200,000 for single filers or $250,000 for married couples filing join tly.[70]

Understanding these numbers matters because they determine your true take-home income. If you're charging clients the same hourly rate you earned as an employee, you've effectively given yourself a pay cut of roughly 7.65%—the employer half you're now covering yourself. This is why experienced freelancers build their rates to account for both halves of self-employment tax, plus the cost of benefits they formerly received from employers. Your pricing strategy and your retirement planning are inseparable. You can't save adequately for retirement if you're not charging enough to cover your true tax burden first.

Strategic Deductions for Independent Contractors: Home Office, Mileage, and Business Expenses That Reduce Taxable Income

The most powerful tax-reduction strategy available to independent contractors isn't exotic or complicated; it's simply claiming the deductions you're already entitled to. Yet I've watched countless freelancers leave thousands of dollars on the table every year because they either don't know that these deductions exist or they're afraid that claiming them will trigger an audit. Let me be clear: legitimate business deductions aren't red flags. They're rights built into the tax code specifically for people like us who work for themselves.

The Home Office Deduction: Your Biggest Missed Opportunity

If you work from home regularly and exclusively in a dedicated space, even a corner of a room, you likely qualify for the home office deduction.[75 76] The IRS requires that the space be used regularly and exclusively for business, and that it serves as your principal place of b usiness.[75 76] For most freelancers whose administrative work happens at home, this test is easily met, even if you perform services at client locations.

You have two calculation methods. The simplified method gives you $5 per square foot of office space up to 300 square feet, for a maximum deduction of $1,500 annually. It requires virtually no record-keeping beyond measuring your space. The actual expense method lets you deduct the business-use portion of your rent, mortgage interest, utilities, insurance, repairs, and property taxes. If you're paying $1,800 monthly rent and your 150-square-foot office represents 12% of your 1,250-square-foot apartment, you can deduct $2,592 annually just from rent, plus your proportional share of utilities, renters' insurance, and internet service.

For someone earning $70,000 in net self-employment income, a $4,000 home office deduction saves approximately $1,020 in combined self-employment and income taxes.[74] That's money you can redirect straight into your Solo 401(k).[74 29]

Mileage: The Deduction That Adds Up Fast

Business mileage is one of the largest deductions most independent contractors can claim, yet many freelancers track it haphazardly or not at all. The IRS standard mileage rate for 2024 is 67 cents per mile. If you drive to client meetings, coworking spaces, networking events, or to purchase supplies, those miles are deductible. Personal commuting, driving from home to a regular workplace, doesn't count, but here's the advantage of a qualifying home office: travel from your home office to client sites is considered business travel, not commuting.

Track every business trip with a simple log noting the date, destination, purpose, and miles driven. If you drive 4,000 business miles annually, that's a $2,680 deduction at the 2024 rate—saving you roughly $685 in taxes. Over a decade, that's nearly $7,000 you've kept instead of sending to the IRS, and that doesn't even account for what those dollars could grow to in your retirement accounts.

Business Expenses: Document Everything

Ordinary and necessary business expenses are fully deductible, and the definition is broader than most freelancers realize. Software subscriptions, professional development courses, business insurance, website hosting, advertising costs, office supplies, professional fees for legal or accounting services, and even 50% of business meals with clients or potential clients; all reduce your taxable income.[75 76]

The key is systematic documentation. Use a dedicated business credit card or checking account to separate business expenses from personal spending. Save receipts digitally using a phone app or cloud storage. Categorize expenses monthly rather than scrambling at tax time.

A freelancer earning $80,000 who properly documents $8,000 in business expenses beyond the home office and mileage deductions will save approximately $2,040 in taxes.[74] Combined with the other deductions we've discussed, you're potentially keeping $3,700 more of your earnings annually, enough to make substantial retirement contributions that will compound over decades into real financial security.[74 29]

Coordinating Retirement Contributions with Tax Planning: Using Solo 401(k) and SEP-IRA Contributions to Lower Your Tax Bill While Building Wealth

The most powerful wealth-building strategy available to self-employed workers isn't complicated; it's coordinating your retirement contributions with your tax planning so that every dollar you save for retirement simultaneously reduces your current tax bill. This isn't about finding loopholes or pushing ethical boundaries. It's about understanding that the tax code specifically rewards retirement savings, and as a freelancer, you have access to contribution strategies that many traditional employees can only dream about.

Here's how the coordination works in practice. When you contribute to a Solo 401(k) or SEP-IRA using pre-tax dollars, you're reducing your adjusted gross income for the year.[77 80 29] That contribution doesn't just build your retirement account; it also lowers the income that's subject to federal and state income tax.[77 80] For someone in the 22% federal tax bracket, a $10,000 retirement contribution saves approximately $2,200 in federal income tax, plus whatever your state tax rate adds. You've essentially received a $2,200 discount on building $10,000 in retirement wealth.

The math becomes even more compelling when you consider the double benefit. That $10,000 contribution will grow tax-deferred for decades, potentially becoming $30,000 or $50,000 by retirement, depending on your timeline and investment returns.[77 80] Meanwhile, the $2,200 you saved in taxes can be redirected, either into additional retirement savings or into your emergency fund, further strengthening your financial position. This is why I always tell freelancers that retirement contributions aren't an expense; they're a tax-advantaged investment in your future that pays dividends immediately.

The key difference between Solo 401(k) and SEP-IRA for tax planning purposes comes down to contribution mechanics and flexibility. A SEP-IRA allows you to contribute up to 25% of your net self-employment earnings, with a maximum of $69,000 for 2024.[80 29] The calculation is straightforward but limited by that percentage formu la.[77 80 29] If your net earnings are $60,000, your maximum SEP-IRA contribution is $15,000, which would save you roughly $3,825 in federal taxes at the 22% bracket plus self-employment tax considerations.

A Solo 401(k) offers more sophisticated tax planning opportunities because you can contribute in two ways: as the employee (salary deferrals up to $23,000 for 2024, or $30,500 if you're 50 or older) and as the employer (up to 25% of compensation).[77 79 80] This dual structure means you can potentially contribute more at lower income levels than you could with a SEP-IRA.[77 78 79 80] If you're earning $50,000 in net self-employment income, you could contribute the full $23,000 employee deferral plus roughly $9,300 as an employer contribution—a total of $32,300 compared to the $12,500 maximum you'd get with a SEP-IRA at that income level.

The catch-up contributions available in Solo 401(k) plans for those age 50 and older create an especially powerful tax-planning tool for freelancers in their peak earning years.[77 78 80 81] That extra $7,500 annually in contributions translates to roughly $1,650 in immediate tax savings at the 22% bracket—money that would otherwise go to the IRS but instead builds your retirement security.

The strategic timing matters too. You can establish a Solo 401(k) by December 31st and make employee deferrals for that tax year, but employer contributions can be made up until your tax filing deadline, including extensions.[29] This flexibility lets you see your full year's income and tax situation before finalizing your contribution strategy, allowing you to optimize the balance between current tax reduction and retirement savings based on your actual financial picture rather than January projections that may not reflect your year-end reality. Tax planning for self-employed workers isn't something that happens once a year when you file your return; it's an ongoing strategy that directly determines how much wealth you can build for retirement. Every dollar you unnecessarily send to the IRS is a dollar that can't compound and grow in your retirement accounts for the next twenty or thirty years. The difference between a freelancer who understands tax planning and one who doesn't isn't just a few thousand dollars in annual savings; it's potentially tens of thousands of dollars in retirement wealth over a career.

The self-employment tax burden is real, and it's substantial. Paying both halves of Social Security and Medicare taxes means you're starting with a 15.3% disadvantage compared to your former employee self. But understanding this reality is the first step toward managing it effectively. You can't build adequate retirement savings if you're not pricing your services to account for your true tax burden, and you can't keep more money for retirement if you don't understand where your money is going.

The deductions available to independent contractors—home office, mileage, business expenses—aren't optional extras or risky audit triggers. They're legitimate tax-reduction strategies that the tax code specifically allows for self-employed workers. A freelancer who properly claims a $4,000 home office deduction, tracks $2,680 in business mileage, and documents $8,000 in business expenses is keeping roughly $3,700 more of their earnings annually compared to someone who ignores these deductions. Over a decade, that's $37,000 that could be building retirement wealth instead of unnecessarily funding the IRS.

But the most powerful coordination happens when you understand how retirement contributions and tax planning work together. Every dollar you contribute to a Solo 401(k) or SEP-IRA using pre-tax dollars simultaneously builds your retirement account and reduces your current tax bill. This double benefit—immediate tax savings plus decades of tax-deferred growth—is the closest thing to free money that exists in personal finance. A $20,000 annual retirement contribution saves approximately $5,100 in taxes for someone in the 22% bracket when you account for both income tax and self-employment tax considerations. You're essentially getting a 25% discount on building retirement wealth.

The key to making all of this work is shifting from reactive to proactive tax management. Set aside 30% of every payment for taxes before you spend anything else. Track every business mile you drive and every business expense you incur throughout the year, not just in March when you're scrambling to file. Coordinate your retirement contributions with your tax situation, making strategic decisions about how much to contribute based on your income, your tax bracket, and your retirement goals.

Tax planning for freelancers isn't about finding loopholes or pushing ethical boundaries; it's about understanding the legitimate strategies that the tax code specifically provides for self-employed workers and implementing them systematically. The government wants to encourage retirement savings and business investment, which is why it makes those activities tax-deductible. But you must know the rules, keep the records, and take actions to benefit from them.

Starting today, implement a year-round tax management system rather than a one-time annual system. Open that separate tax savings account. Download a mileage tracking app. Start documenting your business expenses. Calculate your home office deduction. And most importantly, understand that every dollar you save in taxes through legitimate deductions and strategic retirement contributions is a dollar you're keeping for your future instead of unnecessarily sending to the government. That's not just smart tax planning, it's essential retirement planning for anyone building wealth without an employer to guide them.

Chapter Seven

Social Security Timing and Withdrawal Sequencing for Maximum Freelancer Financial Independence

Ella had circled her 62nd birthday on the calendar in red marker, counting down the months until she could finally claim Social Security and add that monthly check to her freelance income. Then her financial advisor asked her a question that changed everything: "What if waiting eight more years to claim at 70 could increase your monthly benefit by 77% for the rest of your life?"

For most self-employed workers, the decision of when to claim Social Security feels straightforward: take it as soon as you're eligible at 62 and get your money while you can. After years of paying both the employee and employer portions of Social Security taxes, watching 15.3% of your self-employment income disappear into the system, you've earned those benefits. Why wait?

But the timing of your Social Security claim is one of the most consequential financial decisions you'll make as a freelancer, directly affecting not just how much you receive monthly, but how long your retirement savings will last, how much you'll pay in taxes, and whether you'll qualify for healthcare subsidies before Medicare. Unlike traditional employees who might have pensions or employer-sponsored retiree health benefits to bridge the gap, self-employed workers must strategically coordinate their Social Security timing with their retirement account withdrawals to create a sustainable income stream that lasts throughout retirement.

This chapter tackles two interconnected decisions that can make or break your retirement security: when to claim Social Security benefits and how to sequence withdrawals from your different retirement accounts to minimize taxes and maximize the longevity of your savings. These aren't separate choices; they're pieces of the same puzzle that must fit together based on your unique circumstances as an independent worker.

The math behind Social Security timing is more complex than it appears at first. Claiming at 62 gives you money immediately but permanently reduces your monthly benefit by 25-30% compared to waiting until your full retirement age of 67. Delaying until 70 increases your benefit by 24% beyond full retirement age; a guaranteed return that's hard to match anywhere else. But waiting means funding more years entirely from your retirement savings, which could deplete your accounts faster and leave you vulnerable if you live longer than expected.

The decision on withdrawal sequencing is equally critical. You've likely accumulated money in different types of accounts: traditional retirement accounts where withdrawals are taxable, Roth accounts where qualified withdrawals are tax-free, and possibly regular taxable investment accounts. The order in which you tap these accounts dramatically affects how much you pay in taxes, whether you qualify for healthcare subsidies before age 65, and how much wealth you preserve for your later retirement years when you might need it most.

For self-employed workers without the safety net of employer benefits, these decisions require a coordinated strategy that accounts for irregular income history, variable expenses, and the reality that you're building this plan entirely on your own. You can't afford to leave money on the table by claiming Social Security at the wrong time or withdrawing from the wrong accounts in the wrong order.

This chapter will walk you through the specific calculations you need to make based on your age, health, savings level, and income needs. You'll learn how to determine your personal break-even point for Social Security claiming, how to sequence withdrawals to minimize your lifetime tax bill, and how to coordinate these decisions with your healthcare costs before Medicare. Most importantly, you'll discover that these timing decisions aren't about following generic rules; they're about creating a personalized strategy that maximizes your financial independence throughout a retirement that could last thirty years or more.

The Social Security Claiming Decision: Understanding How Age 62, 67, and 70 Affect Your Monthly Benefit and Lifetime Payout

Let's start with the numbers that matter most to you as a self-employed worker. Your Social Security benefit is calculated using your highest thirty-five years of earnings[83], which means all those years of paying both the employee and employer portions of Social Security taxes—that 15.3% self-employment tax—are building toward a specific monthly payment amount.

For someone born in 1960 or later, your full retirement age is sixt y-seven.[83 86] That's the age at which you receive one hundred percent of your calculated benefit.[85] But you can claim as early as sixty-two or delay until seventy[83 85], and each choice creates a dramatically different monthly payment that lasts for the rest of your life.

If you claim at sixty-two, you'll receive approximately seventy percent of your full retirement age benefit, a thirty percent permanent reduction.[83 84 85] Using real numbers: if your full retirement age benefit would be two thousand dollars monthly, claiming at sixty-two drops that to about fourteen hundred dollars.[84] That's seven hundred dollars less every single month for the rest of your life. Over twenty years, that's 168,000 dollars in lost benefits.

Waiting until seventy works in the opposite direction. For each year you delay past your full retirement age, your benefit increases by roughly eight percent annually through delayed retirement credits.[83 85] Waiting from 67 to 70 adds approximately 24% to your monthly payment.[83] That same two-thousand-dollar benefit becomes twenty-four hundred eighty dollars; an extra four hundred eighty dollars monthly, or five thousand seven hundred sixty dollars annually.

The range from 62 to 70 represents a 77% difference in monthly income. Social Security's own materials illustrate this starkly: claiming decisions can mean the difference between $750 and $1,320 monthly for the same work history.[87]

Here's where the lifetime calculation gets tricky. Claiming early gives you more checks but smaller amounts. Delaying gives you fewer checks but larger amounts. The break-even point—where waiting catches up to early claiming—typically falls around age seventy-nine to eighty-two, depending on which ages you're comparing.[82]

If you claim at sixty-two versus waiting until sixty-seven, you'll break even around age seventy-nine.[82] If you live past seventy-nine, waiting would have given you more total lifetime benefits. Die before seventy-nine, and claiming early would have paid out more total dollars.

The sixty-two versus seventy comparison has a break-even age around eighty to eighty-one.[82] The sixty-seven versus seventy comparison breaks even around age eighty-two to eighty-three.[82]

For freelancers, this decision intersects with three critical factors that traditional employees don't face as acutely. First, you're funding your own retirement entirely; there's no pension to supplement a reduced Social Security check. Second, you likely need to bridge healthcare costs before Medicare at sixty-five, which affects how much you can afford to withdraw from retirement savings while delaying Social Security. Third, your earnings history might be more variable than traditional employees[83], meaning your benefit calculation could be lower or higher depending on whether your peak earning years are recent or decades past.

The claiming decision also affects your withdrawal strategy from retirement accounts. If you claim Social Security at sixty-two, you'll need smaller withdrawals from your Solo 401(k) or SEP-IRA to cover expenses. If you delay until 70, you'll need larger withdrawals over those eight years, potentially depleting your accounts faster, but creating a larger guaranteed income floor for your later retirement years when you might not be able to supplement with freelance work.

This isn't a decision you can make in isolation; it's interconnected with every other retirement planning choice you'll make as a self-employed worker.

Withdrawal Sequencing Strategy: Which Accounts to Tap First to Minimize Taxes and Preserve Wealth

The order in which you withdraw money from your retirement accounts matters just as much as when you claim Social Security—and for freelancers juggling multiple account types without employer guidance, getting the sequence wrong can cost you tens of thousands of dollars in unnecessary taxes over your retirement.

Most self-employed workers accumulate money in three distinct buckets, each with different tax treatment. You are likely to have taxable accounts, regular brokerage or savings accounts where you've already paid income tax on the money you deposited. You probably have tax-deferred accounts like a Solo 401(k), SEP-IRA, or traditional IRA, where contributions reduced your taxes when you made them, but withdrawals will be fully taxable. And you might have tax-free Roth accounts, where you pay taxes upfront, but qualified withdrawals are tax-free.

The conventional wisdom suggests a simple order: spend taxable accounts first, then tax-deferred, and save Roth accounts for last.[88 90] This approach preserves tax-advantaged growth for as long as possible and reduces the tax drag from taxable accounts that are subject to annual tax on dividends and interest.[89 90] For many retirees, this sequence works reasonably well and can extend portfolio longevity by several years compared to randomly tapping accounts.[89]

But conventional wisdom was designed for traditional employees with pensions and steady income, not for freelancers with variable earnings history and the flexibility to engineer low-income years. As a self-employed worker, you have unique opportunities to deviate strategically from the standard sequence and save substantially more in lifetime taxes.[91]

The most powerful opportunity comes in those early retirement years before Social Security begins and before Required Minimum Distributions kick in at age seventy-three. If you retire or semi-retire in your early sixties, you might have several years with unusually low taxable income; maybe just twenty to thirty thousand dollars from part-time freelance work and small portfolio withdrawals.[89 90 91 92] These low-bracket years are golden opportunities to intentionally withdraw extra money from your traditional IRA or Solo 401(k), or to convert traditional balances to Roth accounts, while you're in the twelve or twenty-two percent tax bracket instead of waiting until Required Minimum Distributions force you into higher brackets later.[89 91 92]

Let me show you what this looks like with real numbers. Say you're sixty-three, fully retired from your freelance consulting business, and living on forty-five thousand dollars annually. You could withdraw that entire amount from your taxable brokerage account, following the conventional sequence. But if you're married, filing jointly in 2024, you could have up to about $94,000 in taxable income and still stay in the 12% federal bracket. That means you have roughly forty-nine thousand dollars of "room" in that low bracket that you're not using.

Instead of leaving that room empty, you could withdraw an extra twenty thousand dollars from your traditional IRA—paying just twelve percent federal tax on it—and either spend it, save it in taxable accounts for future years, or convert it to a Roth IRA.[89 91 92] When Required Minimum Distributions begin forcing withdrawals at seventy-three, you'll have a smaller traditional IRA balance, which means smaller required distributions that are less likely to push you into higher brackets or trigger higher Medicare premiums.[89 91 92]

This strategy—sometimes called "bracket filling"—flips the conventional sequence on its head during low-income years.[89 91 92] You're intentionally accelerating tax-deferred withdrawals to take advantage of low rates now, rather than deferring them until rates might be higher. For freelancers who can control their income timing, this approach can save twenty to forty thousand dollars in lifetime taxes compared to rigidly following the taxable-first rule.[91]

Coordinating Social Security Timing with Retirement Account Withdrawals and Healthcare Subsidies for Maximum Financial Efficiency

The real power of coordinated planning emerges when you understand how these three decisions—Social Security timing, withdrawal sequencing, and healthcare subsidies—interact to amplify or undermine one another. For freelancers without employer benefits, getting this coordination right can mean the difference between a comfortable retirement and constant financial stress.

Let's start with the healthcare subsidy piece, because it's the most time-sensitive and often the most misunderstood. If you retire before age sixty-five, you'll need individual health insurance through the Affordable Care Act marketplace. Your eligibility for premium tax credits—subsidies that can reduce your monthly insurance cost from fifteen hundred dollars to three hundred dollars or less—depends entirely on your Modified Adjusted Gross Income.

Here's where the coordination gets critical: MAGI includes withdrawals from your traditional Solo 401(k) or SEP-IRA, the taxable portion of Social Security benefits, and any Roth conversions you make. It doesn't include withdrawals from Roth IRAs or the return of principal from taxable accounts. This creates a strategic opportunity that traditional employees with pensions rarely have.

If you retire at sixty-two but delay claiming Social Security until sixty-seven, you have five years to carefully manage your MAGI to maximize healthcare subsidies. During those years, you'd fund your living expenses primarily from Roth withdrawals and taxable account principle, neither of which increases your MAGI, while taking only enough from traditional retirement accounts to stay within the optimal income range for subsidies.

Let me show you what this looks like with actual numbers. Say you're single, need forty-eight thousand dollars annually to live, and your state's marketplace offers strong subsidies for incomes between twenty thousand and fifty-two thousand dollars. You could structure your withdrawals as twenty-five thousand dollars from your Roth IRA, fifteen thousand from taxable accounts, and eight thousand from your traditional IRA. Your MAGI would be just eight thousand dollars, qualifying you for maximum subsidies that could save you twelve thousand dollars annually on health insurance premiums.

But if you claimed Social Security at sixty-two—adding roughly twenty thousand dollars in mostly taxable benefits—your MAGI would jump to around twenty-five thousand dollars, reducing your subsidies significantly.[93] Over those five years before Medicare, that premature Social Security claim could cost you thirty thousand dollars or more in lost subsidies, completely negating the benefit of claiming early.

The coordination extends beyond sixty-five when Medicare begins. Medicare Part B and Part D premiums include Income-Related Monthly Adjustment Amounts, surcharges based on your income from two years prior. A large traditional IRA withdrawal or Roth conversion at age sixty-three will increase your Medicare premiums at age sixty-five. This two-year lookback means you need to start planning your withdrawal strategy before you even retire.

The optimal pattern for many freelancers looks like this: from sixty to sixty-two, make strategic Roth conversions while you're in low tax brackets but before ACA subsidies matter. From sixty-two to sixty-five, minimize MAGI to maximize healthcare subsidies by living primarily off Roth and taxable accounts. At sixty-five, enroll in Medicare[93] and resume moderate traditional IRA withdrawals, staying below IRMAA thresholds. At sixty-seven to seventy, claim Social Security for maximum lifetime benefits[93], then adjust your withdrawal strategy to account for that new guaranteed income stream.

This isn't theoretical optimization; it's practical coordination that can preserve fifty to seventy-five thousand dollars over your first decade of retirement. For self-employed workers, building retirement security entirely on their own, that's real money that extends how long your savings last.

Conclusion: Building Your Coordinated Timing Strategy

The decisions you make about Social Security claiming and withdrawal sequencing aren't separate line items on a retirement checklist—they're interconnected pieces of a financial puzzle that must fit together based on your unique circumstances as a self-employed worker. Unlike traditional employees who might have pensions or employer guidance to simplify these choices, you're building this strategy entirely on your own, which means understanding how each decision amplifies or undermines the others.

The seventy-seven percent difference between claiming Social Security at sixty-two versus seventy isn't just about monthly payment amounts; it's about how much you'll need to withdraw from your retirement accounts during those eight years, how long your savings will last, and whether you'll have enough guaranteed income in your eighties when freelance work is no longer an option. The break-even age of seventy-nine to eighty-two matters, but so does your health, your family longevity history, and your ability to fund those extra years without depleting your portfolio at the worst possible time.

Your withdrawal sequencing strategy isn't about rigidly following the conventional taxable-first rule, it's about recognizing the unique opportunities you have as a freelancer to engineer low-income years, fill up tax brackets strategically, and coordinate your withdrawals with healthcare subsidies before Medicare. Those early retirement years when you're not yet claiming Social Security and not yet facing Required Minimum Distributions are golden opportunities to convert traditional retirement money to Roth accounts while you're in the twelve or twenty-two percent bracket, setting yourself up for more tax-free income later when you might need it most.

The healthcare subsidy coordination is where these strategies either work together brilliantly or fall apart completely. Claiming Social Security at sixty-two might feel like the safe choice, but if it costs you thirty thousand dollars in lost ACA subsidies over three years, you've negated the entire benefit of claiming early. Living off Roth withdrawals and taxable account principal during your early sixties isn't just about tax efficiency, it's about preserving subsidy eligibility that can save you more than a thousand dollars monthly on health insurance.

I learned these lessons the hard way during my own freelance years, watching the interplay between irregular income, tax planning, and retirement timing create either opportunities or obstacles depending on whether I understood the connections. The freelancers who built the most secure retirements weren't necessarily the ones who earned the most, they were the ones who understood that timing decisions compound over decades, and getting the sequence right matters as much as the individual choices themselves.

Your coordinated timing strategy should account for three critical factors that traditional retirement advice often ignores. First, your irregular income history as a freelancer means your Social Security benefit might be lower than someone with steady corporate earnings, making the decision to delay even more impactful. Second, your lack of employer-sponsored retiree health benefits means the years from sixty to sixty-five require careful MAGI management that traditional employees never face. Third, your ability to control income timing through strategic withdrawals gives you flexibility that pension recipients don't have, but only if you understand how to use it.

The roadmap forward isn't about following generic claiming ages or rigid withdrawal sequences. It's about calculating your personal break-even point based on your health and longevity expectations, modeling different scenarios that account for your actual savings level and income needs, and building flexibility into your plan so you can adjust as circumstances change. These timing decisions will shape your financial security for the next thirty years. They deserve the same careful attention you gave to building your freelance business in the first place.

Chapter Eight

Catch-Up Strategies: Accelerated Gig Worker Wealth Building When You're Starting Late

Phoebe sat in her home office at age 47, staring at the retirement account balance she had built over three years: $23,000. Meanwhile, her former college roommate—who'd spent the last two decades in corporate jobs with automatic 401(k) contributions and employer matches—had just casually mentioned her retirement balance had crossed $380,000. Phoebe's story isn't unique, it's the reality for millions of self-employed workers who spent their twenties and thirties building businesses, surviving economic downturns, paying off student loans, or simply not knowing where to start with retirement planning. If you're reading this chapter in your forties or fifties with less saved than you'd hoped, you're not alone, and more importantly, you're not out of options.

The financial industry loves to showcase the power of compound interest by showing how someone who starts saving at 25 can retire a millionaire with modest contributions. Those charts are mathematically accurate, but they're also psychologically devastating if you're 47 and just getting started. What those charts don't show is that late starters have advantages that early savers don't: higher earning potential, clearer understanding of actual expenses, and the life experience to distinguish between what truly matters and what's just noise.

This chapter addresses the elephant in the room that most retirement guides ignore: what do you do when you've "missed" the first fifteen or twenty years of saving? The answer isn't to panic, give up, or resign yourself to working until you're 75. The answer is to implement aggressive, focused strategies specifically designed for people who need to accelerate their wealth building without the luxury of decades of compound growth.

You'll learn how to leverage catch-up contribution limits that become available at age 50—limits that allow you to save significantly more than younger workers or traditional employees. These aren't loopholes or tricks; they're provisions built into the tax code specifically because lawmakers recognized that many people start saving seriously in their forties and fifties. As a self-employed worker, you can combine these catch-up limits with the already-generous contribution limits for Solo 401(k)s and SEP-IRAs to create a wealth-building engine that can accumulate substantial savings in ten to fifteen years.

We'll tackle the uncomfortable truth about aggressive savings rates, that catching up requires saving 25% to 40% of your income, not the 10% to 15% that early savers can get away with. But we'll also show you how to implement these rates without destroying your current quality of life, by strategically cutting expenses that don't truly matter while protecting the things that do. You'll see how to coordinate these higher savings rates with the irregular income patterns that define freelance work, ensuring you can maintain momentum even during lean months.

Perhaps most importantly, this chapter introduces the concept of the semi-retirement bridge, a strategy where you work aggressively in your fifties to build your retirement accounts, then transition to part-time work in your early sixties rather than retiring completely. This approach extends your wealth-building timeline, reduces the number of years you need to fund entirely from savings, and allows you to delay claiming Social Security for a significantly higher monthly benefit. For many late starters, semi-retirement isn't a compromise; it's a better outcome than traditional retirement because it provides both financial security and continued purpose.

Starting late isn't ideal, but it's not hopeless either. With the right strategies, focused execution, and realistic expectations about what's achievable in the time you have, you can still build meaningful retirement security. The key is to stop comparing yourself to people who started at 25 and instead focus on maximizing the specific advantages and opportunities available to you right now, at whatever age you're starting.

Catch-Up Contributions After 50: Maximizing the Extra $7,500 in Solo 401(k)s and Additional IRA Limits

When I turned 50, I discovered something that felt almost too good to be true: the government would let me save an extra $7,500 per year in my Solo 401(k) beyond the standard limits.[95 96 23 98] This wasn't a loophole or a trick. It was a provision built into the tax code specifically for people like me who'd spent their younger years building a business instead of building retirement savings. The catch-up contribution rules are Congress's acknowledgment that many workers, especially self-employed ones, need a way to accelerate their savings in their final working years.[96]

Here's how the numbers work for 2025. If you're under 50, you can contribute up to $23,500 in employee deferrals to your Solo 401(k).[95 96 98] Once you turn 50, you can add an extra $7,500 in catch-up contributions, bringing your total employee deferral to $31,000.[95 96 23 98] And here's the crucial part that many freelancers miss: this is just the employee portion. You can still make employer contributions on top of that, typically around 20% of your net self-employment income if you're a sole proprietor, or 25% of your W-2 wages if you've incorporated.[94 96 27]

The total you can contribute to a Solo 401(k) in 2025, including both employee and employer contributions plus catch-up, can reach $77,500 if you're 50 or older and have sufficient income.[96 23] For someone earning $85,000 in net self-employment income, that might look like $31,000 in employee deferrals (including the $7,500 catch-up) plus roughly $17,000 in employer contributions, totaling $48,000 into your retirement account in a single year.

But there's a significant change coming in 2026 that affects higher earners. Under the SECURE 2.0 Act, if your prior-year wages from your business exceeded $150,000, your catch-up contributions must be made to a Roth Solo 401(k) rather than the traditional pre-tax version.[94 95 97 99] This means you'll pay taxes on that $7,500 now, but it will grow tax-free, and you won't owe taxes when you withdraw it in retirement. If your Solo 401(k) doesn't offer a Roth option, you won't be able to make catch-up contributions at all once this rule takes effect.[94]

For freelancers earning less than $150,000, which includes most of us, you'll still have the choice between traditional pre-tax catch-up contributions and Roth catch-up contributions.[94 95] The decision depends on whether you'd rather reduce your tax bill now or create tax-free income in retirement.

You can also combine Solo 401(k) catch-up contributions with IRA catch-up contributions if you're eligible.[97] Traditional and Roth IRAs have their own catch-up provision for people 50 and older, allowing additional contributions beyond the standard IRA limit .[97] Using both accounts simultaneously can accelerate your savings even faster, though you'll need to navigate the income limits and deductibility rules that apply to IRAs.

The key to maximizing catch-up contributions with irregular freelance income is treating them as non-negotiable rather than optional. In a strong earning year, fully fund your catch-up contributions before spending on anything discretionary. In a lean year, contribute what you can; even $2,000 in catch-up contributions is $2,000 more than you had before. The mistake many late-starting freelancers make is waiting for the "perfect" year when they have plenty of extra money. That year rarely comes. Instead, build catch-up contributions into your percentage-based savings system from the moment you turn 50, making them as automatic as your tax payments.[96 97 98]

These catch-up provisions aren't just about numbers; they're about possibility. They're the difference between resigning yourself to working until 70 and actually retiring at 65. They're the mechanism that lets you compress fifteen years of missed savings into ten focused years of aggressive contributions.[96] And for self-employed workers who've spent decades building businesses instead of retirement accounts, they're exactly the tool you need to catch up without giving up.

The Aggressive Savings Rate Strategy: How to Save 30-40% of Income When You're Starting Late Without Destroying Your Current Quality of Life

When I finally sat down to calculate what I needed to save to catch up, the number made me nauseous: 35% of my gross income. For years, I'd been proud of myself for saving 12%, thinking I was being responsible. But the retirement calculator didn't care about my feelings; it just showed me the math.[100] If I wanted to retire at 65 with anything resembling security, I needed to nearly triple my savings rate. The question wasn't whether I should do it, but whether I could do it without living on ramen and giving up everything that made life worth living.

The brutal truth about aggressive savings rates is that they require aggressive action. You cannot ease into saving 30-40% of your income the same way you might gradually increase from 5% to 10%. The gap is too large, and if you're starting in your forties or fifties, you don't have time for incremental changes.[100] [1] But here's what I learned: aggressive doesn't have to mean miserable. It means strategic, focused, and intentional about where every dollar goes.

Start by separating your expenses into three categories: non-negotiable essentials, valued priorities, and everything else. Your non-negotiables are housing, basic food, essential transportation, health insurance, and minimum debt payments, the things that keep you alive and legally solvent.[1] For most freelancers, this is 50-60% of income. Your valued priorities are the expenses that genuinely contribute to your quality of life, maybe that's your gym membership that you actually use three times a week, your weekly coffee shop work session that doubles as social time, or your annual camping trip with friends. These might be 10-15% of your income.

Everything else—and this is where most people discover they have more room than they thought—is negotiable. The streaming services you barely watch. The subscription boxes that seemed fun but now feel like clutter. The convenience purchases that add up to hundreds monthly. The restaurant meals that happen because you're tired, not because you're enjoying them.[100 1] When I did this exercise honestly, I found nearly $800 monthly in spending that brought me zero joy and minimal convenience.

Here's the framework that made 35% savings achievable for me: I committed to protecting my valued priorities while ruthlessly eliminating the "everything else" category. I kept my coworking space membership because working around other people genuinely improved my mental health and productivity. I kept my monthly dinner with my freelancer friends because that social connection mattered. But I canceled four streaming services, started meal planning to cut my grocery bill by 30%, switched to a cheaper phone plan, and stopped buying books I never read.[100] These weren't painful sacrifices; they were eliminating waste I hadn't even noticed.

The second critical piece is timing your aggressive savings to your income peaks. With irregular freelance income, you cannot save the same dollar amount every month.[1 101] Instead, implement a tiered system: in months when you earn your baseline amount, save 25%. In months when you exceed your average by 20% or more, push your savings rate to 40-50% of that excess income.[1] This approach lets you average 30-35% annually without starving yourself during slower months.

Finally, automate everything possible.[100 1] The moment a client payment hits your account, automatically transfer your target percentage to your retirement account before you can rationalize spending it.[100 1] Treat your savings like a non-negotiable bill, because it is.[1 101] You're paying your future self, and that bill comes due whether you're ready or not. The aggressive savings rate isn't about deprivation, it's about making a focused, time-limited push to build the security you need, while protecting the things that actually matter to your quality of life right now.

The Semi-Retirement Bridge: Using Part-Time Gig Work to Extend Your Wealth-Building Timeline and Reduce How Much You Need to Save

When I turned 52, I made a decision that confused everyone who knew me: instead of planning to work full-time until 67, I started planning to work part-time until 72. My friends thought I was extending my working years, but math told a completely different story. By shifting to semi-retirement at 60 and continuing to earn just $25,000 annually through selective freelance projects, I could retire with $200,000 less in savings than I'd need for a traditional retirement at 60 with no income.

The semi-retirement bridge isn't about working longer; it's about working smarter during the years when most people are either grinding full-time or withdrawing heavily from their portfolios. For late starters, this strategy can be more powerful than trying to save every possible dollar in your final full-time working years, because even modest ongoing income dramatically changes how much capital you need.[103]

Here's the math that changed my perspective. If you need $50,000 annually to live and you retire completely at 60, you need your portfolio to generate that entire amount for potentially 30-40 years. Using a conservative 3.5% withdrawal rate for early retirement, that requires roughly $1.4 million saved. But if you can earn $20,000 annually from part-time gig work from age 60 to 70, you only need your portfolio to provide $30,000 during those ten years. That drops your required savings to approximately $850,000, a difference of $550,000.

The beauty of this approach for gig workers is that you already have the infrastructure. You have clients who value your work, skills that command market rates, and experience managing irregular inco me.[102] Semi-retirement doesn't mean starting from scratch; it means being selective. Instead of taking every project that comes your way, you take the two or three annually that pay well, interest you, and fit your schedule.

I've watched this play out with dozens of freelancers in my network. One graphic designer I know transitioned at 58 from working 40-50 hours weekly to working roughly 15 hours weekly on retainer for her two favorite clients. She earns $28,000 annually, covers most of her basic expenses, and barely touches her retirement accounts. Her portfolio has grown during her "retirement" years because she's withdrawing so little while markets have been favorable. Another consultant friend works intensively for three months each year on a single major project, earning $35,000, then travels and pursues hobbies the other nine months.

The key is choosing gig work that scales with your energy and capacity. Knowledge-based work, consulting, writing, design, bookkeeping, tutoring, and coaching tend to be sustainable into your sixties and seventies because they don't require physical stamina.[103] [104] One freelance editor I know is 68 and still takes on manuscript projects, working maybe 10-12 hours weekly and earning $18,000 annually. That income alone delays her need to claim Social Security and reduces her portfolio withdrawals by more than half.

This strategy also gives you greater flexibility than pure retirement. If markets crash early in your semi-retirement, you can temporarily increase your gig hours to reduce portfolio withdrawals during the downturn.[102 103] If you have an expensive year—major home repair, family emergency, health issue—you can take on an extra project rather than depleting your savings. And if you discover you genuinely love full retirement, you can always stop the gig work entirely once your portfolio has had more years to grow.

For late starters who feel behind, semi-retirement isn't a compromise; it's often the most realistic path to financial security. You're not extending your working life; you're extending your wealth-building timeline while simultaneously reducing how much wealth you need to build.[103] That combination can turn an impossible savings target into an achievable one.

Moving Forward: Your Catch-Up Plan Starts Today

If you've reached this chapter feeling behind on retirement savings, you now understand something crucial: starting late doesn't mean starting hopeless. The strategies in this chapter, catch-up contributions after 50, aggressive savings rates of 30-40%, and the semi-retirement bridge, aren't theoretical concepts. They're practical tools that thousands of self-employed workers have used to transform seemingly impossible retirement goals into achievable realities within ten to fifteen focused years.

The catch-up contribution limits available at age 50 exist specifically because lawmakers recognized that many people, especially those building businesses, start saving seriously in their forties and fifties. That extra $7,500 annually in your Solo 401(k), combined with the already-generous employer contribution limits available to self-employed workers, creates a wealth-building engine that can accumulate substantial savings even when you're starting decades later than the financial magazines suggest you should have. This isn't a consolation prize; it's a genuine advantage that traditional employees with standard 401(k)s don't have access to.

The uncomfortable truth about catching up is that it requires aggressive action. Saving 10% or 15% of your income won't close the gap when you're starting at 47 or 52. You need to save 25% to 40% for a concentrated period, and that requires making real choices about what expenses truly contribute to your quality of life versus what you've been spending out of habit. But aggressive doesn't mean miserable. By protecting your valued priorities while eliminating the waste you haven't even noticed, you can achieve these savings rates without destroying what makes your current life worth living.

The semi-retirement bridge might be the most powerful strategy in this chapter because it fundamentally changes the equation. Instead of trying to save enough to fund 30 years of complete retirement, you extend your wealth-building timeline while simultaneously reducing how much wealth you need to build. Earning even $20,000 to $30,000 annually from selective freelance projects in your early sixties can reduce your required retirement savings by hundreds of thousands of dollars. For gig workers, this isn't starting a new career; it's simply being selective about the work you already know how to do.

Here's what matters most: you need to start implementing these strategies now, not when conditions are perfect or when you've figured out every detail. Open that Solo 401(k) this week if you haven't already. Calculate your actual expenses and identify where you can cut without genuine sacrifice. Commit to a specific savings percentage and automate the transfers before you can rationalize spending the money elsewhere. Every month you delay is a month of compound growth you'll never get back.

The comparison to friends who started saving at 25 will always sting a little. But that comparison is also irrelevant. You're not trying to match their wealth. You're trying to build enough for your own secure retirement using the time and resources you actually have. The catch-up strategies in this chapter give you the tools to do exactly that. Whether you're 45 or 55, whether you have $20,000 saved or $200,000, the question isn't whether you should have started earlier. The question is what you're going to do with the years you have left. And now you know exactly how to answer that question with focused action instead of regret.

Chapter Nine

Early Retirement Strategies and Sustainable Withdrawal Plans for the Self-Employed

Jasmine had finally done it. At 56, after building her freelance consulting business for eighteen years, she had $680,000 saved and was ready to retire early. But three months into retirement, watching her portfolio drop 12% during a market correction while she withdrew money for living expenses, she realized that early retirement wasn't just about having enough money; it was about having a withdrawal strategy that could survive the worst-case scenarios. The dream of leaving the workforce before 65 is particularly appealing to self-employed workers who've spent decades managing the stress of irregular income, chasing clients, and handling every aspect of their businesses on their own. But early retirement for freelancers and gig workers comes with unique challenges that traditional retirement guides rarely address. Challenges that can derail even the most carefully calculated plans if you don't understand what you're up against.

Unlike traditional employees who might have retiree health benefits or the option to claim a pension at 55, self-employed workers face a critical gap between their desired retirement age and when safety nets like Medicare and full Social Security benefits become available. If you retire at 58, you're looking at seven years of paying for individual market health insurance before Medicare kicks in at 65, insurance that can cost $1,200 to $1,800 monthly or more as you age. You're also facing the decision of whether to claim reduced Social Security benefits at 62 or delay claiming to receive higher monthly payments later, all while your retirement savings must cover 100% of your living expenses with no employer pension to supplement your income.

The withdrawal strategies that work for someone retiring at 65 with Social Security already flowing and Medicare covering healthcare costs simply don't translate to early retirement scenarios. The famous 4% rule—which suggests you can safely withdraw 4% of your portfolio annually—was designed for 30-year retirements starting at traditional retirement age. But if you're retiring at 56 or 58, you could be looking at a 35 or 40-year retirement, which requires a more conservative approach and far more flexibility than a fixed percentage can provide. Add in the sequence-of-returns risk, the danger that market downturns in your early retirement years can permanently damage your portfolio's ability to sustain you, and early retirement becomes a complex puzzle that requires specialized strategies.

This chapter will show you how to build sustainable withdrawal plans specifically designed for self-employed early retirees. You'll learn why the standard 4% rule often fails for freelancers retiring before 65, and what withdrawal rates make sense when you're facing decades of retirement without employer benefits. We'll explore the critical concept of sequence-of-returns risk and why the timing of market downturns matters just as much as average returns over your retirement. You'll discover variable withdrawal strategies that adapt to market conditions, protecting your portfolio during downturns while allowing you to enjoy gains in good years.

Most importantly, you'll learn how to coordinate multiple income sources—retirement account withdrawals, part-time freelance income, Social Security timing, and healthcare subsidies—into a cohesive early retirement bridge that gets you from your last day of full-time work to the security of Medicare and Social Security without depleting your savings. Early retirement for the self-employed isn't about having a massive nest egg that makes work optional forever; it's about building flexible systems that make full-time work optional while preserving your wealth throughout a potentially very long retirement.

The Early Retirement Withdrawal Challenge: Why the 4% Rule Doesn't Work for Self-Employed Workers Retiring Before 65

The 4% rule has become retirement planning gospel. Withdraw 4% of your portfolio in your first year of retirement, adjust that dollar amount for inflation each year, and your money should last 30 yea rs.[105 108 109] It's simple, memorable, and dangerously misleading for self-employed workers retiring before 65.

I learned this the hard way when I first started planning my own early retirement. I'd calculated that with $500,000 saved, I could withdraw $20,000 annually (4%) and feel secure. The math seemed solid until I started mapping out the actual years between age 58 and when Medicare would kick in at 65. Those seven years of paying $1,400 monthly for health insurance alone would consume $117,600, nearly a quarter of my nest egg, before I'd even covered food, housing, or utilities. The 4% rule suddenly looked like a fantasy designed for someone with very different circumstances than mine.

Here's what the 4% rule assumes, and why each assumption breaks down for early-retiring freelancers:

The 30-Year Horizon Problem: The original research behind the 4% rule tested whether portfolios could survive 30 years of withdrawals based on historical market returns.[105 107 109] If you retire at 65 and live to 95, that's exactly 30 years.[105 109] But retire at 55 and live to 95? That's 40 years, a full decade longer that dramatically increases the odds your portfolio will fail.[12 106] Research suggests that for retirements lasting 40-50 years, safe withdrawal rates drop to 3% or even lower.[107] That means the same $500,000 portfolio should only generate $15,000 annually, not $20,000, a 25% reduction in available income.

The Social Security Gap: Traditional retirees at 65 typically start claiming Social Security within a few years, which reduces how much they need to withdraw from their portfolios. The 4% rule implicitly assumes this income supplement will arrive relatively soon.[105 108] But if you're 56 and planning to delay Social Security until 67 or 70 to maximize your benefit, you're looking at 11-14 years of covering 100% of your expenses from your portfolio alone. During those years, you're not really withdrawing 4%, you're effectively withdrawing 6% or 7%

because there's no Social Security income reducing your portfolio dependence.

The Healthcare Cost Explosion: The 4% rule was developed assuming relatively predictable expenses that increase with general infla tion.[105 107 109] But healthcare costs for individuals in their late 50s and early 60s don't follow general inflation; they explode.[105] A 58-year-old paying $1,600 monthly for marketplace insurance is spending $19,200 annually on premiums alone, before deductibles or out-of-pocket costs. For someone with a $400,000 portfolio, that's nearly 5% of their nest egg going to healthcare alone, leaving almost nothing for the rest of life's expenses if they're trying to stick to a 4% total withdrawal rate.

Sequence-of-Returns Risk Hits Harder: The 4% rule assumes you'll stick to your inflation-adjusted spending regardless of market performance.[105 108 109] But when you retire early and immediately face a market downturn—like a 20% drop in your first two years—you're withdrawing money from a shrinking portfolio.[108] This "sequence-of-returns risk" is devastating for early retirees because you have more years ahead for the damage to compound. A traditional 65-year-old retiree facing the same downturn has Social Security starting soon, and a shorter horizon; an early retiree has neither.

The bottom line: the 4% rule isn't wrong for everyone, but it's specifically wrong for self-employed workers retiring before 65.[106] You need withdrawal strategies that account for longer horizons, healthcare gaps, and the absence of employer safety nets, strategies we'll build in the sections ahead.

Sequence of Returns Risk and Variable Withdrawal Strategies: Protecting Your Portfolio in the Critical Early Years

The sequence-of-returns risk isn't some abstract academic concept; it's the difference between a comfortable 30-year retirement and running out of money at 72. Here's what makes it so dangerous: two retirees can have identical portfolios, earn the same average returns over 20 years, and end up with completely different outcomes based solely on when those returns happened.[110 111 112 113]

Let me show you what I mean by real numbers. Imagine two freelancers, both retiring at 58 with $600,000 saved. Both withdraw $30,000 annually (5% initially), and both experience the exact same returns over the next decade, just in different orders. Freelancer A gets strong returns in years 1-5 (averaging 8% annually) and weak returns in years 6-10 (averaging 2% annually). Freelancer B gets the same returns, but in reverse: weak returns first, strong returns later.

After ten years, Freelancer A has approximately $520,000 remaining. Freelancer B? Only $440,000—$80,000 less despite identical average returns and identical withdrawals.[110 112 113] That $80,000 gap exists purely because of the sequence—the order in which the returns arrived. Freelancer B's portfolio suffered weak returns while at its largest, and those withdrawals during the downturn permanently reduced the base that could benefit from the later recovery.[111 113]

This is why the first decade of retirement is often called the "fragile decade." Research shows that roughly 77% of your final retirement outcome can be explained by what happens in your first ten years of withdrawals.[111] If you retire into a bear market and keep withdrawing money while your portfolio drops, you're selling shares at depressed prices and leaving fewer assets to participate in the eventual recovery .[111 113] The damage compounds over decades.

For self-employed workers retiring before 65, this risk is amplified because you're facing a longer retirement horizon—potentially 35 or 40 years instead of 30—and you're fully dependent on your portfolio with no pension to cushion the blow.[111] You can't afford to just hope the sequence works in your favor.

Variable withdrawal strategies offer protection by making your spending responsive to market conditions, rather than rigidly sticking to a fixed dollar amount regardless of what's happening to your portfolio. The core principle is simple: withdraw less when markets are down, withdraw more when they're up.[111 113] This flexibility dramatically reduces the risk of depleting your portfolio during a bad sequence.

One practical approach is the **guardrails method**. Set a target withdrawal rate—say 4% of your portfolio—but establish upper and lower boundaries. If your portfolio drops significantly and your withdrawal rate exceeds 5% of your current balance, cut spending by 10-15% until you're back within the guardrails. If your portfolio grows and your rate falls below 3%, you can increase spending modestly. This prevents you from withdrawing too aggressively during downturns while allowing you to enjoy gains in good years.

Another strategy is the **percentage-of-portfolio approach**: instead of withdrawing a fixed dollar amount, you withdraw a set percentage of your current portfolio value each year, perhaps 3.5% to 4.5%. If your portfolio drops from $600,000 to $500,000, your withdrawal automatically drops from $24,000 to $20,000. Yes, your income fluctuates, but your portfolio is protected from the devastating combination of market losses and rigid withdrawals.[111 113]

For freelancers, the most powerful variable strategy combines flexible withdrawals with flexible work. In years when your portfolio takes a hit, you reduce discretionary spending and pick up some freelance projects to cover the gap. You're not going back to full-time work; you're doing enough to avoid withdrawing from a depressed portfolio. This approach leverages the advantage you have over traditional retirees: marketable skills and the ability to control your work schedule.

Building Your Early Retirement Bridge: Coordinating Multiple Income Sources, Healthcare Costs, and Flexible Withdrawal Rates for Long-Term Sustainability

The real power of early retirement for self-employed workers isn't in having one massive pile of money; it's in orchestrating multiple income sources that work together like instruments in a band, each playing its part at the right time. I learned this while mapping out my own early retirement at 58. I'd been so focused on hitting my portfolio number that I'd missed the bigger picture: my retirement didn't need to be funded solely by withdrawals.

Think of your early retirement bridge as having three distinct phases, each with its own income mix. **Phase One** runs from your retirement date until you claim Social Security, let's say ages 58 to 67. During these years, you're combining modest portfolio withdrawals with part-time freelance income and possibly rental income or other passive sources. **Phase Two** begins when Social Security starts, but before Medicare kicks in, maybe just one or two years if you time it right. **Phase Three** begins at 65, when Medicare dramatically reduces your healthcare costs, freeing up cash flow previously consumed by insurance premiums.

The key is matching each income source to the phase where it makes the most sense. During Phase One, prioritize withdrawals from taxable investment accounts rather than tax-deferred retirement accounts. Why? Because withdrawals from regular brokerage accounts give you more control over your taxable income, which directly affects your eligibility for ACA marketplace health insurance subsidies. If you can keep your Modified Adjusted Gross Income below certain thresholds—$60,000 for a single person in 2024, for example—you might qualify for premium tax credits that reduce your monthly insurance costs from $1,600 to $400 or less.

This is where freelance income becomes a strategic tool rather than a means to fail at retirement. Let's say your annual expenses are $48,000, but you can earn $18,000 from occasional consulting projects, maybe 15 hours per week for six months of the year. That means you only need to withdraw $30,000 from your portfolio, rather than $48,000. Over a nine-year bridge to Social Security, that's $162,000 less withdrawn from your investments, leaving substantially more money to compound and grow.

But here's the critical coordination point: you need to balance that freelance income against your healthcare subsidy eligibility. Earn too much, and you lose subsidies that might be worth $10,000 annually. The sweet spot is often earning just enough to reduce portfolio withdrawals while staying within subsidy thresholds. For many early retirees, this means targeting $15,000 to $25,000 in annual freelance income, enough to meaningfully reduce portfolio stress without triggering subsidy cliffs.

Your withdrawal strategy during the bridge years should be explicitly tied to market conditions. In years when your portfolio gains 15% or 20%, you can withdraw more aggressively—maybe 4.5% to 5% of your portfolio—and skip some freelance work. In years when markets drop 10%, you cut discretionary spending, withdraw only 3% or less, and pick up an extra project or two.[116] This flexibility is your advantage as a self-employed worker: you can dial your income up or down based on need.

The healthcare piece deserves its own line item in your bridge bud get.[115] From 58 to 65, budget $1,200 to $1,800 monthly for individual insurance premiums, plus another $3,000 to $5,000 annually for deductibles and out-of-pocket costs. That's $17,400 to $26,600 per year just for healthcare, potentially 35% to 55% of a modest retirement budget. This is why managing your income to maximize subsidies isn't optional; it's essential to making early retirement sustainable.

When Social Security begins in Phase Two, your portfolio withdrawal needs drop dramatically. That $2,400 monthly Social Security check covers half your expenses, meaning you're only withdrawing $1,000 to $1,200 monthly from investments. And when Medicare starts at 65, your healthcare costs might drop from $1,600 monthly to $400 or less, freeing up another $14,400 annually. Suddenly, your portfolio withdrawals become minimal, giving your investments room to recover and grow for your later years.

This coordinated approach—flexible work, strategic withdrawals, subsidy management, and phased income sources—transforms early retirement from a high-risk gamble into a sustainable system that adapts to whatever markets and life throw at you.[114] [115] [116]Early retirement for self-employed workers isn't about reaching some magical number that makes work optional forever, it's about building systems flexible enough to survive decades of uncertainty while giving you the freedom to choose how much you work. Jasmine's story illustrates what thousands of freelancers discover when they retire before 65: the withdrawal strategy matters just as much as the accumulation strategy, and sometimes more.

The 4% rule that dominates retirement planning conversations was never designed for someone retiring at 56 with no pension, no employer health benefits, and potentially 40 years of expenses to fund. When you're self-employed and retiring early, you need withdrawal rates closer to 3% to 3.5%, variable strategies that adapt to market conditions, and the willingness to earn some income during your early retirement years when your portfolio needs protection. This isn't failure, it's smart risk management that leverages the marketable skills you've spent decades developing.

Sequence-of-returns risk stops being an abstract concept the moment you retire into a market downturn and watch your portfolio shrink as you withdraw money for groceries and health insurance. Those first 10 years of retirement will largely determine whether your money lasts 30 or 50 years, which is why variable withdrawal strategies aren't optional for early retirees; they're essential. The guardrails method, percentage-of-portfolio withdrawals, and flexible spending tiers all serve the same purpose: protecting your portfolio during the fragile decade when damage is hardest to recover from.

Building your early retirement bridge means coordinating multiple moving parts that traditional retirees never have to think about. You're managing portfolio withdrawals to minimize taxes, earning enough freelance income to reduce portfolio stress without losing healthcare subsidies, timing Social Security to maximize lifetime benefits, and budgeting $17,000 to $26,000 annually just for healthcare until Medicare arrives at 65. Each decision affects the others, which is why early retirement for the self-employed requires active management rather than a set-it-and-forget-it autopilot.

The healthcare gap between your retirement date and Medicare eligibility at 65 deserves its own dedicated planning because it can easily consume 30% to 50% of a modest retirement budget. Managing your income to stay eligible for ACA marketplace subsidies isn't gaming the system; it's using the tools available to make early retirement financially sustainable. A $1,600 monthly premium that drops to $400 through subsidies saves you $14,400 annually, which is the difference between a 4% withdrawal rate and a 6% rate for someone with a $400,000 portfolio.

Part-time freelance work during your early retirement years isn't an admission of defeat; it's the strategic advantage that self-employed workers have over traditional retirees. Earning $15,000 to

$25,000 annually from occasional projects you enjoy means withdrawing $15,000 to $25,000 less from your portfolio during the critical years when sequence-of-returns risk is highest. Over a decade, that's $150,000 to $250,000 less portfolio depletion, which translates to substantially more wealth preserved for your later years when you might not be able to work at all.

Early retirement before 65 is achievable for self-employed workers, but it requires abandoning the fantasy of never working again and embracing the reality of flexible retirement, where work becomes optional rather than mandatory. You're not trying to accumulate enough money to fund 40 years of expenses at a fixed withdrawal rate. You're building a system that combines modest portfolio withdrawals, strategic part-time income, optimized Social Security timing, and careful healthcare management into a sustainable bridge that gets you from your last day of full-time work to the security of Medicare and Social Security without depleting your savings. That's not compromise, that's smart planning for the long journey ahead.

Chapter Ten

Your Personalized Freelance Retirement Roadmap: Putting It All Together

Olivia spread nine years of tax returns across her dining room table, along with bank statements, retirement account summaries, and a notebook filled with calculations she'd made while reading through retirement planning guides. She'd absorbed an overwhelming amount of information about Solo 401(k)s, healthcare subsidies, withdrawal strategies, and Social Security timing, but now she faced the hardest question of all: where did she actually start?

If you're feeling like Olivia—simultaneously informed and paralyzed—you're not alone. Throughout this book, we've covered retirement numbers and account types, tax strategies and healthcare planning, Social Security timing, and withdrawal sequencing. Each chapter provides specific strategies for self-employed workers, freelancers, and gig economy professionals. But knowing what to do and implementing a cohesive plan are two very different challenges.

This is where most retirement planning books leave you hanging. They provide information but not integration. They explain individual strategies but don't show you how to coordinate them into a personalized roadmap that reflects your actual income, your real expenses, and your specific circumstances. They assume you'll somehow figure out which strategies to prioritize, which actions to take first, and how to adapt the plan as your freelance business and life circumstances inevitably change.

This chapter is different. We're going to take everything you've learned and transform it into a practical, personalized action plan you can start implementing today. Not someday when conditions are perfect or when you've figured out every detail, today, with whatever income level, savings balance, and life situation you currently have.

The truth is that successful retirement planning for self-employed workers isn't about perfection. It's not about implementing every possible strategy simultaneously or following some rigid sequence of steps that work for everyone. It's about understanding where you are right now, defining where you need to be, and building a flexible roadmap with clear milestones that create momentum without overwhelming you.

We'll start by helping you honestly assess your current situation, not where you wish you were or where you think you should be, but where you are. Then we'll work through a framework for prioritizing actions based on your age, income level, and existing savings. You'll learn how to break your retirement plan into manageable phases: what to focus on in the next 90 days, what goals to target over the next 12 months, and what objectives to work toward over the next five years.

Most importantly, you'll discover how to build flexibility into your plan so it can adapt as your freelance income fluctuates, your business evolves, and your life circumstances change. Because here's what traditional retirement planning guides miss: self-employed workers don't have the luxury of set-it-and-forget-it automatic payroll deductions. Your income varies month to month. Your business priorities shift. Your personal circumstances evolve. Your retirement plan needs to work with that reality, not against it.

By the end of this chapter, you won't just understand retirement planning concepts, you'll have your own personalized roadmap with specific next steps. You'll know exactly which retirement account to open (if you haven't already), how much to save based on your current income, which tax strategies to implement first, and how to coordinate healthcare planning with your retirement timeline. You'll have a clear path forward that's tailored to your situation as a self-employed worker, not some generic plan designed for corporate employees with steady paychecks and employer benefits.

The mountain of information that felt overwhelming when you started this book is about to become a manageable series of concrete actions. Let's build your roadmap.

Creating Your Personal Retirement Roadmap: A Step-by-Step Framework for Prioritizing Actions Based on Your Age, Income, and Current Savings

Your retirement roadmap isn't a single document; it's a framework that adapts to three critical factors: your age, your income level, and how much you've already saved. Let's break down how to prioritize your actions based on where you are right now.

If You're Under 35 with Little to No Retirement Savings

Your biggest advantage is time, but your biggest challenge is probably inconsistent income and competing financial pressures.[1] Here's your priority sequence:

Start by building a basic cash buffer of $2,000 to $3,000 before making retirement contributions your primary focus. This isn't a full emergency fund yet; it's just enough to prevent one bad month from derailing everything.[1] Once you have that buffer, implement a percentage-based savings system: set aside 25% of every payment for taxes and 10% for retirement, even if that 10% is only $50 some months.[114] [118]

Open a Roth IRA as your first retirement account.[117] [114] At lower income levels early in your career, paying taxes now and getting tax-free growth for 30-plus years is almost always the better choice.[117] You can contribute up to $7,000 annually (2024 limit), and if you can't hit that target, contribute whatever you can consistently manage.[1] [114]

Your investment strategy should be aggressive: 90% to 100% in stocks through low-cost index funds.[1] You have decades to ride out market volatility, and conservative investments at this age actually increase your risk of not having enough later.

If You're 35-50 with Moderate Savings ($20K-$150K)

You're in the critical acceleration phase. Your income is likely more stable than it was in your twenties, but you're also facing peak expenses, maybe a mortgage, kids, or aging parents. Your priorities shift.

First, calculate your actual retirement number using the methods from Chapter 2. You need a concrete target, not a vague sense that you should "save more."[1] If that number feels overwhelming, remember you're not trying to save it all tomorrow, you're building a system that will get you there over 15 to 30 years.

Next, evaluate whether you're using the right retirement accounts. If you're still contributing to a Traditional IRA but your income has grown to $75,000 or more, a Solo 401(k) likely makes more sense because of the higher contribution limits.[117 114] You can contribute up to $69,000 annually as both employee and employer (2024 limits), far more than the $7,000 IRA limit.[117]

Your target savings rate should be 15% to 20% of gross incom e.[114 118] If you're currently saving less, increase by 2% to 3% every six months until you hit that range. This gradual approach is more sustainable than trying to jump from 5% to 20% overnight, which can burn you out.

Your investment mix should shift slightly more conservative, maybe 80% stocks and 20% bonds, but you still need significant growth exposure.[1 117] You're not close enough to retirement to prioritize safety over growth.

If You're Over 50 with Any Savings Level

Time is now your constraint, which means your actions need to be more aggressive and more strategic. The good news: you're eligible for catch-up contributions once you turn 50, an extra $7,500 annually in a Solo 401(k) and $1,000 in an IRA.

Your first priority is to get brutally realistic about your retirement timeline and the income you need. If you have $100,000 saved at age 52 and need $1 million by age 65, you'll need to save approximately $40,000 annually, assuming a 7% return. If that's not feasible with your current income, you have three options: increase income, reduce retirement expenses, or work longer than 65.

Consider the semi-retirement bridge strategy: plan to work part-time from 62 to 67 rather than retiring completely. This extends your savings timeline, reduces how much you need to withdraw from retirement accounts, and allows you to delay claiming Social Security for a significantly higher benefit.[1]

Your investment allocation should gradually shift toward 60% stocks and 40% bonds as you approach retirement, but don't abandon growth entirely.[1] [117] You potentially have 30-plus years of retirement to fund.

The framework isn't about perfection; it's about matching your actions to your actual situation and adjusting as circumstances change.

The 90-Day Action Plan: Immediate Steps Every Self-Employed Worker Can Take This Quarter to Start Building Retirement Security

The most effective retirement plan is worthless if you never implement it. That's why this 90-day action plan breaks down your first quarter of retirement building into specific tasks you can schedule right now, not someday when conditions are perfect, but this week.

Days 1-7: The Foundation Week

Your first action happens today, before you finish this chapter: open a high-yield savings account separate from your regular checking. Label it "Tax & Retirement Buffer." This single account will hold money for two purposes: quarterly estimated taxes and retirement contributions. By Friday of this week, transfer $500 into this account if you can, or $100 if that's what's realistic for your current situation. The amount matters less than establishing the account and making that first transfer.

Next, calculate your baseline monthly expenses, the absolute minimum you need to survive.[120] Include rent, utilities, food, insurance, and debt payments. Exclude everything else for now. Write this number down. This is your emergency fund target: three months' worth of this baseline.[120] If you don't have this saved yet, your 90-day goal is to build toward it while simultaneously starting retirement contributions, splitting your available savings between the two.[120]

By day seven, schedule a recurring calendar event called "Financial Review" for every Friday at the same time for the next 13 weeks. [119] Block thirty minutes. This weekly appointment with yourself is non-negotiable.

Days 8-30: Account Setup and Automation

Week two is account-opening week. If you earned more than $20,000 last year from self-employment, open a Solo 401(k) with a low-cost provider like Vanguard, Fidelity, or Charles Schwab.[120] The application takes twenty to forty minutes online. If you earned less than $20,000 or want to start simpler, open a Roth IRA instead; it has lower contribution limits but requires less paperwork.[120]

Don't overthink investment choices during setup. Select a target-date fund that matches when you turn 65. These funds automatically adjust from aggressive to conservative as you age. You can refine your investment strategy later; right now, the priority is getting the account open and funded.

By day twenty-one, implement your contribution system. Here's the formula that works with irregular income: every time a client's payment hits your account, immediately transfer 30% to your Tax & Retirement Buffer account before you spend anything else. When that buffer account reaches $2,000, make your first retirement contribution of $1,000. Then let it rebuild to $2,000 and contribute another $1,000. This rhythm ensures you're never caught short on taxes while steadily building retirement savings.[120]

Days 31-60: Optimization and Habit Building

Month two focuses on increasing the money available for saving without earning more. Review your last three months of bank and credit card statements.[120] Identify your three largest discretionary expense categories, typically dining out, subscriptions, or shopping. Cut one completely for the next sixty days and reduce another by half. Redirect that money to your buffer account.

This is also when you contact your three best clients to discuss a rate increase. Even a 10% increase in your top clients can add $400 to $800 to your monthly savings capacity. Send the emails this week; implement the new rates for any work starting after day sixty.[119]

Days 61-90: Assessment and Acceleration

Your final month is about measurement and momentum. By day seventy-five, calculate your actual retirement contributions for the quarter. If you've contributed less than $1,500, identify what blocked you: insufficient income, unexpected expenses, or lack of discipline? Adjust your system accordingly.

By day ninety, set your target for quarter two: increase your contribution rate by 2% to 5%. If you save 10% of income this quarter, aim for 12% to 15% next quarter.[120] Small, consistent increases compound dramatically over time.

The 90-day plan isn't about perfection; it's about establishing the systems that make retirement saving automatic rather than aspirational.[120] Start today.

Building Flexibility into Your Plan: How to Adapt Your Retirement Strategy as Your Freelance Income, Life Circumstances, and Goals Change Over Time

The retirement roadmap you create today won't be the same roadmap you follow in five years, and that's exactly how it should be. Unlike traditional employees whose retirement plans can run on autopilot through automatic payroll deductions, freelancers need plans that breathe, flex, and adapt to the constant changes that define self-employment.[1]

I learned this the hard way during my third year of freelancing, when I'd meticulously planned to save $1,200 a month for retirement. Then two major clients delayed payments by sixty days, a third project fell through entirely, and suddenly, my beautiful plan was worthless. I had two choices: abandon retirement savings completely that quarter, or build a more realistic system that worked with my actual income patterns rather than my aspirational ones.

The Three-Tier Flexibility Framework

The most sustainable approach to freelance retirement planning uses three distinct savings tiers that automatically adjust to your income reality. Think of these as gears you shift between based on your current circumstances, not failure points when you can't hit your ideal target.

Your baseline tier applies during lean months when income drops below your minimum threshold, maybe $4,000 if your typical expenses run $3,500 monthly. During baseline months, commit to saving just 5% to 8% of income for retirement. This might only be $200 to $320, but maintaining the habit matters more than the amount. You're keeping the system alive even when conditions are tough.

Your standard tier kicks in during normal months when income covers expenses with some breathing room—perhaps $5,000 to $8,000 monthly. Here, you implement your target savings rate of 15% to 20%. This is where most of your retirement building happens, the steady accumulation that compounds over years.

Your acceleration tier activates during abundant months when income significantly exceeds your needs, anything above $8,000 in this example. During these months, save 30% to 40% of income for retirement, or even more if you're playing catch-up.[121 1] These windfall months are your opportunity to make up for leaner times and push your retirement timeline forward.

The beauty of this system is that you never face the binary choice of "save my target amount or save nothing." You're always saving something appropriate to your current reality, which means you maintain momentum even through income fluctuations.[121] [1]

Annual Recalibration Points

Build formal review points into your calendar every six months.[1] [122] During these reviews, ask yourself four specific questions:

Has my average monthly income changed by more than 15% in either direction? If so, recalculate your three-tier thresholds. What counted as "abundant" when you earn $60,000 annually needs adjustment when you're earning $80,000.

Have my essential expenses shifted significantly?[1] [122] A move to a different city, a change in health insurance costs, or paying off a car loan all warrant recalculating your baseline tier threshold.

Has my target retirement age changed?[121] [122] If you've decided to work until 67 instead of 62, or if you're now considering semi-retirement at 60, your required annual savings rate changes accordingly. Recalculate and adjust your standard tier percentage.

Am I still using the right retirement accounts for my income level?[1] [123] If your income has grown from $45,000 to $75,000, switching from a SEP-IRA to a Solo 401(k) might now make sense because of higher contribution limits.

When Life Demands Major Pivots

Some circumstances require temporarily suspending retirement contributions entirely, such as a medical crisis, caring for a family member, or rebuilding after your business takes a serious hit.[1] [122] This isn't failure; it's reality. The key is defining clear conditions for when you'll resume contributions. "When things get better" is too vague. "When my emergency fund reaches $5,000 again" or "when my monthly income stabilizes above $4,500 for three consecutive months" gives you a concrete restart point.[1 122]

Your retirement plan isn't a rigid contract; it's a living framework that evolves as your freelance journey unfolds.[121] [1]Olivia's dining room table is clear now. The overwhelming stacks of tax returns, the confusing account statements, the notebook filled with crossed-out calculations—all of it has been distilled into something manageable: a single-page roadmap with three actions for the next ninety days, four goals for the next twelve months, and three objectives for the next five years. That transformation from paralysis to clarity is exactly what happens when you stop trying to implement every strategy simultaneously and start building a plan that matches your actual situation.

Your retirement roadmap doesn't need to be perfect. It needs to be yours. Tailored to your real income, your actual expenses, your specific age, and your unique circumstances as a self-employed worker. The freelancer earning $45,000 annually needs a different roadmap than the one earning $95,000. The 28-year-old just starting out faces different priorities than the 52-year-old playing catch-up. And that's exactly the point: retirement planning for self-employed workers isn't about following someone else's predetermined path. It's about creating your own path based on where you are right now and where you need to go.

Throughout this book, you've learned the specific strategies that work for freelancers, gig workers, and independent contractors, people who fund their own retirement without employer matches, navigate irregular income without automatic payroll deductions, and bridge the healthcare gap without retiree benefits. You've discovered how to calculate your personal retirement number. Choose between Solo 401(k)s and SEP-IRAs, build wealth despite variable cash flow, plan for healthcare before Medicare, and optimize taxes while maximizing retirement contributions. Time Social Security strategically, implement catch-up strategies when starting late, create sustainable withdrawal plans for early retirement, and coordinate all these elements into a cohesive strategy.

But information without implementation is just entertainment. The difference between freelancers who successfully build retirement security and those who remain perpetually anxious about their future isn't knowledge—it's action. Specifically, it's taking the first action today, the second action this week, and the third action this month, building momentum through small, consistent steps rather than waiting for perfect conditions that never arrive.

Your ninety-day action plan starts now. Open that separate savings account today. Calculate your baseline expenses this week. Set up your retirement account this month. Implement your percentage-based contribution system before the quarter ends. These aren't aspirational goals for someday; they're concrete actions with specific deadlines that transform retirement planning from an overwhelming concept into a manageable series of tasks you can complete.

Remember that your roadmap will evolve as your freelance business grows, your income changes, and your life circumstances shift. The three-tier flexibility framework ensures you're always saving something appropriate to your current reality, whether you're in a lean month, a normal month, or an abundant month. Your semi-annual review points keep your plan aligned with your actual situation rather than outdated assumptions. And your willingness to adjust strategies as needed means you're building a sustainable system, not following a rigid script that breaks down when reality doesn't cooperate.

The mountain of retirement planning that felt impossible when you started this book is now a series of achievable steps. You know what to do, you know why it matters, and you know how to adapt when circumstances change. The only question left is: when will you take the first step? Not someday when you earn more, not next year when things settle down, not when you finally feel ready. Today. Right now. With whatever income, savings, and situation you currently have. Your freelance retirement starts with that first action, and every action after that builds the financial security you deserve.

Help Other Freelancers Build Wealth

If *Your Freelance Retirement* gave you clarity or confidence, please consider leaving a review. Your honest feedback helps the algorithms recommend this guide to other freelancers, designers, and gig workers who need a better system.

Visit the link below to share your thoughts in less than a minute.
https://www.amazon.com/dp/1971604011

Thank You for Trusting the Process Freelancing requires a special kind of bravery. It takes guts to bet on yourself every single day, without a safety net or a guaranteed paycheck. Thank you for choosing this book to help build your safety net. My hope is that the systems you've learned here give you the freedom to create, work, and live without fear of the future. Here's to retiring on your own terms.

Chapter Eleven

Bonus Content

90-Day Action Plan Checklist: Your Freelance Retirement Roadmap

Days 1–7: The Foundation Week

- [ ] **Open a "Tax & Retirement Buffer" Account**
    - Open a high-yield savings account separate from your regular checking.
    - Label it "Tax & Retirement Buffer." This single account will hold money for two purposes: quarterly estimated taxes and retirement contributions.
- [ ] **Make Your First Transfer**
    - Transfer $500 into this new account by Friday (or $100 if that is your current reality). The habit matters more than the amount.

- [ ] **Calculate Baseline Monthly Expenses**
  - Calculate the absolute minimum needed to survive: rent/mortgage, utilities, food, insurance, and minimum debt payments.
  - Exclude all discretionary spending for this calculation.
- [ ] **Set Emergency Fund Target**
  - Multiply your baseline monthly expense number by three. This is your initial emergency fund goal.
- [ ] **Schedule Your "Financial Review"**
  - Block 30 minutes on your calendar every Friday for the next 13 weeks. Treat this as a non-negotiable client meeting.

Days 8–30: Account Setup and Automation

- [ ] **Choose Your Account Type**
  - If you earned >$20,000 last year: **Solo 401(k)**.
  - If you earned <$20,000 last year or want simplicity: **Roth IRA**.
- [ ] **Open the Account**
  - Apply online with a low-cost provider (e.g., Vanguard, Fidelity, Schwab). This typically takes 20–40 minutes.
- [ ] **Select Initial Investment**
  - Choose a target-date fund that matches the year you turn

65 to automate your risk management.

- [ ] **Implement the 30% Rule**
    - Every time a client payment hits your account, immediately transfer **30%** to your Tax & Retirement Buffer account. Do this before spending a dime.
- [ ] **Set Contribution Trigger**
    - When the buffer account reaches $2,000, transfer $1,000 to your retirement account.
    - Let it rebuild to $2,000, then repeat.

Days 31–60: Optimization and Habit Building

- [ ] **Audit Discretionary Expenses**
    - Review bank statements from the last three months. Identify your three largest discretionary categories (e.g., dining out, subscriptions).
- [ ] **Execute the Cut/Reduce Strategy**
    - Cut one category completely for the next 60 days.
    - Reduce a second category by half.
    - Redirect these savings immediately to your buffer account.
- [ ] **Contact Top 3 Clients**
    - Send emails to your three best clients to discuss a rate increase.

  - Aim for a 10% increase.
  - Implement the new rates for any work starting after Day 60.

Days 61–90: Assessment and Acceleration

- [ ] **Calculate Quarterly Contribution**
  - By Day 75, total up your retirement contributions for the quarter.
- [ ] **Troubleshoot Roadblocks**
  - If you contributed less than $1,500, identify the specific blocker (income, unexpected expense, or discipline) and adjust your system.
- [ ] **Set Quarter 2 Target**
  - Increase your contribution rate by 2% to 5% for the next quarter. (e.g., if you saved 10% this quarter, aim for 12–15% next quarter).

Weekly Friday Financial Review Agenda

Time Required: 30 Minutes **Goal:** Process the week's income, trigger automated transfers, and reset for the week ahead.

1. **Income Processing (10 Minutes)**
   - **Log Payments:** List every client payment received in the last 7 days.

- **Execute the "Tax & Retirement" Transfer:** For every payment received, immediately transfer **30%** to your dedicated "Tax & Retirement Buffer" account.

- **Buffer Check:** Check the balance of your "Tax & Retirement Buffer" account.

    - *The Trigger:* Has it reached **$2,000**?

    - *The Action:* If yes, transfer **$1,000** to your retirement account and leave the remaining $1,000 for taxes.

2. Expense & Tax Maintenance (10 Minutes)

- **Categorize Expenses:** Quickly review your business credit card or checking transactions. Label expenses (software, supplies, meals) now so you aren't scrambling at tax time.

- **Mileage Log:** Update your mileage log for any client meetings or business trips taken this week.

- **Spending Check-in:** Briefly review your personal discretionary spending. Did you stick to the "cut/reduce" strategy you set for this quarter?

3. The "Tier" Check-In (5 Minutes)

- **Identify Your Tier:** Based on the month's total income so far, which savings tier are you in?

    - *Baseline Mode:* Income is low/lean. Focus on maintaining just the habit (5–8% savings).

    - *Standard Mode:* Income is normal. Stick to your target savings rate (15–20%).

    - *Acceleration Mode:* Income is abundant. Push savings to 30–40% of the excess.

- **Adjust:** If you just had a windfall payment, manually move the extra "Acceleration" percentage to savings now.

4. The Look Ahead (5 Minutes)

- **Upcoming Bills:** What large expenses (quarterly taxes, annual software renewals, insurance premiums) are hitting in the next 14 days?
- **Ensure:** Your personal checking or business account has sufficient funds ready.

Chapter Twelve

Jargon-Free Glossary

1099: The tax form for independent contractors describes the "no-benefits" financial reality of freelancers.

4% Rule: Traditional advice to withdraw 4% of savings annually; often insufficient for early-retiring freelancers due to healthcare costs.

ACA (Affordable Care Act): Legislation creating the health marketplace; critical for bridging the gap to Medicare via Premium Tax Credits.

Baseline-Plus Strategy: A savings method: commit to a minimum in lean months, then save a high percentage of "excess" income in good months.

Buffer: A dedicated savings account (distinct from emergency funds) that smooths irregular income into a steady "salary."

Catch-Up Contributions: Extra IRS-allowed retirement contributions for those age 50+ ($7,500 for Solo 401(k)s in 2025).

Healthcare Bridge Fund: A specific savings reserve calculated to cover premiums and out-of-pocket costs between early retirement and age 65.

MAGI (Modified Adjusted Gross Income): The income figure used to determine eligibility for ACA subsidies; managing this is key to lower premiums.

Roth: Accounts funded with post-tax dollars; withdrawals in retirement are tax-free. Ideal for lower income years.

SEP-IRA: A simple, flexible retirement plan for self-employed workers allowing employer-only contributions (approx. 20–25% of net income).

Solo 401(k): A plan for self-employed individuals with no employees; offers the highest contribution limits (employee + employer portions).

Triple Burden: The unique challenge freelancers face: funding their own taxes, healthcare, and retirement simultaneously.

Chapter Thirteen

Bibliography

References

1 Do, B.. (2025, January 6). *Freelancer's Guide to Retirement Planning: Secure Your Future*. Upwork.

[2] Tidwell, J.. (2025, December 5). *How to plan for retirement on a freelance income (5 options)*. Bonsai.

[3] Small Business Majority. (2017, March 22). *Freelancers Need Flexible Retirement Options*. Small Business Majority.

[4] Royal, J.. (2025, May 07). *Best retirement plans for the self-employed*. Bankrate.

[5] Shelton, A.. (2021, July 13). *Freelancers, Sole Proprietors, and Other Nontraditional Workers Have Little Retirement Savings*. The Pew Charitable Trusts.

[6] Donovan, S. A., Li, Z., & Myers, E. A.. (2025, April 7). *Nontraditional Workers and Retirement Saving: An Overview and Discussion of Policy Issues*. Congressional Research Service.

[7] Allchin, L.. (October 16, 2024). *The gig economy and the looming retirement crisis*. RFI Global.

[9] Georgia State University College of Law. (n.d.). *Access Denied - WAF Rule Reached*. Georgia State University Law Review.

[12] Physician Side Gigs. (n.d.). *The 4% Rule for Retirement: Understanding the Basics, Assumptions, and Limitations*. Physician Side Gigs.

[13] Mr. Money Mustache. (2012, May 29). *How Much Do I Need for Retirement?*. Mr. Money Mustache.

[14] Dunleavey, M.. (n.d.). *Beyond the 4% rule: 5 alternative retirement income strategies*. Britannica Money.

[15] Farther. (n.d.). *What Is 4% Rule for Retirement: Does It Still Work?*. Farther.

[16] Williams, R., & Kawashima, C.. (April 15, 2025). *The 4% Rule: How Much Can You Spend in Retirement?*. Charles Schwab.

[17] Choose FI. (n.d.). *Health Insurance For Self-Employed Individuals*. ChooseFI.

[18] Anspach, D.. (March 29, 2022). *How to Plan for Healthcare Costs in Retirement 2022*. Sensible Money.

[19] Gabriel, E.. (2023, October 12). *Calculating How Much To Save For Retirement – The Profit First Method*. DrillDown Solution.

[20] Financial Mentor. (n.d.). *Ultimate Retirement Calculator*. Financial Mentor.

[21] Robertson, S.. (2025, November 18). *401(k) Contribution Limits for 2026, 2025, and More*. ShareBuilder 401k.

[22] Principal. (2025, November 24). *What are 2026 401(k) and IRA max contribution limits?*. Principal.

[23] Mehaffey, S.. (2025, July 22). *Solo 401(k) 2026 Mandatory Roth Requirements for FICA Wages*. EisnerAmper.

[24] Magno, C.. (n.d.). *401(k) contribution limits*. ADP.

[25] Internal Revenue Service. (2025, November 13). *401(k) limit increases to $24,500 for 2026, IRA limit increases to $7,500.* IRS.

[26] MissionSquare. (n.d.). *2026 Retirement Plan Contribution Limits (401k, 457(b) & More).* MissionSquare.

[27] Internal Revenue Service. (2025, August 26). *One-participant 401(k) plans.* Internal Revenue Service.

[28] Roopnarine, M.. (2026, January 1). *Understanding Solo 401(k) Plans [2026].* Scarlet Oak Financial Services.

[29] Internal Revenue Service. (2025, August 26). *Retirement plans for self-employed people.* Internal Revenue Service.

[30] MBO Partners. (2024, October 26). *Is SEP IRA a Good Retirement Option for Self-Employed Professionals?.* MBO Partners.

[31] Edelman Financial Engines. (January 29, 2025). *Saving for retirement with a SEP IRA.* Edelman Financial Engines.

[32] Internal Revenue Service. (2025, August 26). *Simplified Employee Pension plan (SEP).* Internal Revenue Service.

[33] Fidelity Investments. (n.d.). *SEP IRA - Simplified Employee Pension Plan.* Fidelity.

[34] Charles Schwab. (n.d.). *SEP IRA.* Charles Schwab.

[35] U.S. Department of Labor, Employee Benefits Security Administration. (n.d.). *SEP Retirement Plans For Small Businesses.* U.S. Department of Labor.

[36] Ascensus. (n.d.). *SEP IRA featuring Vanguard investments.* Ascensus.

[37] Ameriprise Financial. (n.d.). *Roth IRA benefits: 5 reasons why Roth IRAs can be a powerful investment tool.* Ameriprise Financial.

[38] Charles Schwab. (n.d.). *Roth IRA.* Charles Schwab.

[39] TIAA. (n.d.). *Explore the tax benefits of a Roth IRA.* TIAA.

[40] Fidelity. (2025, October 10). *9 Roth IRA benefits.* Fidelity.

[41] University of Michigan Human Resources. (n.d.). *Roth Options*. University of Michigan Human Resources.

[42] Internal Revenue Service. (2025, August 26). *Roth IRAs*. Internal Revenue Service.

[43] Mutual of America. (n.d.). *Roth IRA Features & Benefits*. Mutual of America.

[44] Thrivent Mutual Funds. (n.d.). *The benefits of opening a Roth IRA*. Thrivent Funds.

[45] Dahle, J.. (2025, February 03). *Comparing Portfolio Withdrawal Strategies in Retirement*. White Coat Investor.

[46] Morningstar. (2026). *What's a Safe Retirement Withdrawal Rate in 2026?*. Morningstar.

[47] BlackRock. (n.d.). *Retirement withdrawal rules and strategies for financial success*. BlackRock.

[48] Beattie, K.. (2025, June 30). *Smart retirement withdrawal strategies for financial stability*. Capital Group.

[49] Solo 401k. (2024, January 24). *Solo 401k Retirement Roadmap for Gig Economy Workers*. Solo 401k.

[50] Morrison, K., & Stueve, C.. (n.d.). *Financial Wellness in the Gig Economy: Empowering Flexibility with Stability*. AFCPE.

[51] AdelFi, a Division of CCCU. (2025, June 3). *Gig Economy Financial Planning: Balancing Flexibility and Faithfulness*. AdelFi Banking.

[52] Suttle Crossland Wealth Advisors. (2025, August 13). *The Gig Economy Retirement Challenge: Building Security Without Traditional Benefits*. Suttle Crossland.

[53] Abojani. (2025, March 21). *Retirement Planning for Freelancers*. Abojani.

[54] Kennedy, R.. (n.d.). *What are the Retirement Plan Options for Freelancers?*. IMPACTfolio.

[55] Lebens Advisory Group. (n.d.). *Retirement Planning for Freelancers*. Lebens Advisory Group.

[56] FreelanceFin. (n.d.). *How to Plan Retirement Freelancer: Securing Your Future, One Contribution at a Time*. FreelanceFin.

[57] Venteur. (n.d.). *How Much Does Individual Health Insurance Cost in 2026?*. Venteur.

[58] Fitzpatrick, M.. (2025, December 29). *How Much Does Health Insurance Cost (2026 Plan Year)*. MoneyGeek.

[59] Darr, M.. (2025, November 10). *Your Guide to the 2026 ACA Health Insurance Market*. StretchDollar.

[60] KFF. (2024, October 29). *Health Insurance Marketplace Calculator*. KFF.

[61] Internal Revenue Service. (2025, November 5). *Eligibility for the Premium Tax Credit*. Internal Revenue Service.

[62] Henry-Moreland, B.. (n.d.). *Reducing ACA Health Insurance Premiums After The Expiration Of The 'Enhanced' Premium Tax Credit*. Kitces.com.

[63] Strike, B.. (October 22, 2025). *Understanding Changes to the Premium Tax Credit*. Mercer Advisors.

[64] Internal Revenue Service. (n.d.). *The Premium Tax Credit – The basics*. Internal Revenue Service.

[65] Collins, R.. (2026, December 30). *Qualifying for Health Insurance Tax Subsidies in Retirement*. Burney Tax Advisors.

[66] Plummer, S.. (December 19, 2025). *7 Ways to Save Money on Bridge Health Insurance While You're Between Jobs or Retire Early*. Annuity Expert Advice.

[67] Retirement Researcher. (n.d.). *Building a Social Security Bridge*. Retirement Researcher.

[68] Sullivan Kilroy, D.. (2025, January 9). *What is a Social Security bridge and do you need one?*. TheStreet.

[69] Averkamp, H.. (n.d.). *What is the self-employed person's FICA tax rate for 2025 and 2026?*. AccountingCoach.com.

[70] NerdWallet. (n.d.). *Self-employment tax: What it is and how to calculate it*. NerdWallet.

[71] Social Security Administration. (n.d.). *Contribution and Benefit Base*. Social Security Administration.

[72] Internal Revenue Service. (2025, November 9). *Self-employment tax (Social Security and Medicare taxes)*. Internal Revenue Service.

[73] CCH AnswerConnect. (n.d.). *Self-employment tax*. CCH AnswerConnect.

[74] Internal Revenue Service. (2025, August 26). *Self-employed individuals: Calculating your own retirement plan contribution and deduction*. Internal Revenue Service.

[75] H&R Block. (n.d.). *Self-employment tax deductions to help your bottom line*. H&R Block.

[76] Mengle, R.. (2025, November 2). *20 Tax Deductions for Self-Employed People*. TurboTax.

[77] Sarcione, K.. (n.d.). *Solo 401(k) vs SEP IRA*. Guideline.

[78] Royal, J.. (2025, July 09). *Solo 401(k) vs. SEP IRA: Comparing retirement plans for entrepreneurs and freelancers*. Bankrate.

[79] Thrivent. (2025, January 8). *Solo 401(k) vs. SEP IRA: Choosing the right retirement plan for your business*. Thrivent.

[80] Farther. (n.d.). *Solo 401(k) vs. SEP IRA: What Is Right for You?*. Farther.

[81] Kiplinger. (n.d.). *SEP IRA vs. Solo 401(k): Which Is Better?*. Kiplinger.

[82] SmartAsset. (n.d.). *Your Social Security break-even age is when waiting to claim yields more total benefits than claiming early, based on lifespan and earnings.*. SmartAsset.

[83] Kirst, G.. (n.d.). *Taking Social Security at 62 vs. 67 vs. 70*. Northwestern Mutual.

[84] Pruitt, P.. (2025, October 06). *Collecting Social Security Benefits at 62 vs. 67 vs. 70*. AARP.

[85] Social Security Administration. (n.d.). *Starting Your Retirement Benefits Early*. Social Security Administration.

[87] Hutchinson, D.. (December 20, 2024). *When to Take Social Security: 5 Key Considerations*. Assembly Wealth.

[88] New York State Deferred Compensation Plan. (n.d.). *What is a withdrawal strategy?*. New York State Deferred Compensation Plan.

[89] Reichenstein, W.. (2006, September 30). *Tax-Efficient Sequencing of Accounts to Tap in Retirement*. TIAA Institute.

[90] French, B.. (n.d.). *Withdrawal Sequencing: Avoiding the Pitfalls of Retirement Distribution Order*. Retirement Researcher.

[91] Young, R., & Reichenstein, W.. (November 2025). *How to make your retirement account withdrawals work best for you*. T. Rowe Price.

[92] Coxwell, K.. (2024, September 5). *How to Decide the Order of Accounts for Retirement Withdrawals: Traditional vs. Other Options*. Boldin.

[94] IRA Financial. (December 11, 2025). *The New 2026 Solo 401(k) Roth Catch-Up Rule: What High-Income Owners Need to Know*. IRA Financial.

[95] Fidelity Investments. (n.d.). *Solo 401(k) Plan | Maximize Retirement Savings | Fidelity Investments*. Fidelity Investments.

[96] Jaiya. (2025, January 6). *How Solo 401k Catch-up Contributions Work*. Carry.

[97] Adams, H.. (December 5, 2025). *Catch-Up Contributions 2025 and 2026*. Charles Schwab.

[98] Droblyen, E.. (2025, October 7). *401(k) Catch-Up Contributions: Final SECURE 2.0 Rules for Employers*. Employee Fiduciary.

[99] Baker Donelson. (2025, November 6). *An Employer's Practical Guide to 401(k) Plan Catch-Up Contribution Changes for 2026*. Baker Donelson.

[100] Aliche, T.. (n.d.). *Catch Up Retirement Savings: 7 Strategies That Actually Work*. The Budgetnista.

[101] ITP Accounting Professionals. (n.d.). *Saving for Retirement as a Freelancer*. ITP Accounting Professionals.

[102] Rich Dad Entrepreneur Team. (2025, August 19). *The Gig Economy Investor: Building Assets While Freelancing*. Rich Dad.

[103] Alden, L.. (n.d.). *How to Build Wealth Fast- This Chart Shows What it Takes*. Lyn Alden.

[104] Casaba, M. G.. (2024, November 17). *Multiple Income Streams: Building Wealth Beyond Your 9-to-5*. Advancing the Seed.

[105] SoFi. (n.d.). *What Is the 4% Rule for Retirement Withdrawals?*. SoFi.

[106] Kiplinger. (n.d.). *The 4% Rule Gets a Closer Look*. Kiplinger.

[107] Dahle, J.. (2025, December 21). *The 4% Rule and Safe Withdrawal Rates*. White Coat Investor.

[108] Haegele, B.. (2025, September 03). *How to use the safe withdrawal rate (SWR) method*. Bankrate.

[109] Motley Fool Wealth Management. (2024, July 10). *Dynamic Spending in Retirement*. Fool Wealth.

[110] MIT Sloan School of Management. (n.d.). *Mitigating sequence of returns risk (SORR)*. MIT Sloan Action Learning.

[111] Schwab Center for Financial Research. (November 7, 2023). *Timing Matters: Understanding Sequence-of-Returns Risk*. Charles Schwab.

[113] Adams, R.. (2025, September 24). *Sequence of Returns Risk: Why Timing Matters*. American Century Investments.

[114] Fox Business. (n.d.). *Review: The Money Book For Freelancers.* Fox Business.

[115] D'Agnese, J., & Kiernan, D.. (June 3, 2006). *The Money Book for Freelancers, Part-Timers, and the Self-Employed: The only personal finance system for people with not-so-regular jobs.* Goodreads.

[116] Covenant Wealth Advisors. (n.d.). *Top 10 Retirement Planning Book Reviews.* Covenant Wealth Advisors.

[117] American Translators Association. (2025, September 25). *Freelancer Retirement Planning: U.S. Accounts and Exit Tips.* American Translators Association.

[118] Black, S.. (2011, February 17). *Review: The Money Book For Freelancers.* Get Rich Slowly.

[119] Gandia, E.. (n.d.). *#361: Your Second Act — Moving From Freelance Success to Significance.* B2B Launcher.

[120] Etsy. (n.d.). *90 Day Tracker.* Etsy.

[121] Bram, T.. (n.d.). *How 2: Set Up a Retirement Plan.* WOW! Women On Writing.

[122] TCWGlobal. (2023, June 5). *Best Ways to Prepare for Retirement as a Freelancer.* TCWGlobal.

[123] Alliance of Independent Authors. (2024, October 7). *Planning for Retirement: Financial Strategies for Indie Authors.* Self-Publishing Advice.

Made in United States
Cleveland, OH
06 November 2026

47647247R00080